A Friedman/Fairfax Book
Friedman/Fairfax Publishers
Please visit the website: *www.metrobooks.com*

This edition published by Friedman/Fairfax by
arrangement with The Ilex Press Limited
2003 Friedman/Fairfax Publishers
Copyright © 2003 The Ilex Press Limited

A CIP record for this book is available from the
Library of Congress

This book was conceived, designed, and produced
by The Ilex Press Limited, The Barn, College Farm,
1 West End, Whittlesford, Cambridge CB2 4LX England
Sales office: The Old Candlemakers, West Street,
Lewes, East Sussex BN7 2NZ England

Publisher: Alastair Campbell
Executive Publisher: Sophie Collins
Creative Director: Peter Bridgewater
Editorial Director: Steve Luck
Art Director: Tony Seddon
Editor: Stuart Andrews
Designer: Jane Lanaway
Development Art Director: Graham Davis

ISBN 1-58663-966-8

Distributed by Sterling Publishing Company, Inc.
387 Park Avenue South
New York, NY 10016

Distributed in Canada by
Sterling Publishing
Canadian Manda Group
One Atlantic Avenue, Suite 105
Toronto, Ontario, Canada M6K 3E7

For up-to-date links and resources, please visit:
www.webexpertseries.com/type

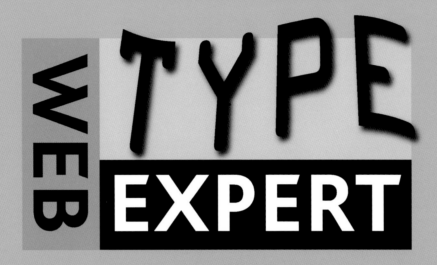

WEB TYPE EXPERT

ALL THAT YOU NEED TO CREATE YOUR

OWN FANTASTIC WEBSITES

TOM ARAH

FRIEDMAN/FAIRFAX

PUBLISHERS

CONTENTS

6

Introduction

Type used to be the domain of master craftsmen. Then with the advent of technologies such as offset printing, hot metal, and the humble typewriter, it became a workaday medium for disseminating the printed word. Today, however, digital technologies, inexpensive software, and the Internet have combined to bring type to life and put it into the hands of everyone to enhance their communication skills. So how do you become a type expert in the online world? Read on...

Potential problems, and practical solutions

The Web, as we know it, may have existed for a mere handful of years in technological terms, but it has already established itself as a medium to rival the printed page. In fact, it can leave the static, printed page looking seriously dated. Simply by publishing a webpage, you can make your message instantly and freely available across the world to anyone, who has access to an Internet connection.

With such immense advantages over the printed page, it's no surprise that the amount of information held on, and communicated over, the Web is enormous and growing exponentially. The vast majority of that information is stored as text. This is why the use of type is such an important element for Web designers to master. But take just a cursory glance at a random selection of the untold billions of webpages out there and it's clear that this it is a discipline used by many, but understood by few.

Typographers and skilled designers differ from people who merely slap down a flashy typeface on the page and think that this is sufficient to attract attention and hold the reader's gaze. Reading is largely a visual act, and the experts recognize that controlling the appearance of text adds to and enhances the message the characters contain.

In the five centuries following the invention of the printing press, typography grew into a fully developed discipline, but one that remained a mystery to all but a small circle of artists, intellectuals, and their patrons. Since the arrival of the home computer, however, a whole world of type creation and control has been opened up to the public. The revolution hit its stride with the introduction of desktop publishing (DTP) in the late 1980s. This gave us a level of typographic power that previous generations could only dream of, and made it available to anyone with access to a computer. Today, as sophisticated software becomes ever more affordable, anyone can be a type expert!

But, like so many things to do with the Web, it's not quite as simple as we would like. The Web is a near-perfect publishing medium. The typographic tools, skills, and knowledge built up over generations of print publishing are there to draw on. The computer has proved itself to be the ideal platform to open up that power to the end user. So what's the problem? Why not simply translate the expert typographical power of DTP to the Web?

The problem (as anyone who has attempted it will know) is that trying to gain mastery over type on a webpage is a completely different proposition to doing so on the printed page. Suddenly, rather than being in complete control of typefaces, layout, size, and spacing, designers find themselves struggling to impose order on factors they would normally take for granted. As many users have realized to their cost, trying to manage type on the Web can, at best, be mildly exasperating, or, at worst, a hair-tearing nightmare.

The good news is that it *is* possible and you *can* take control. There's no instant, one-off solution, but by going back to first principles and understanding both the Web's screen-based nature and the HTML code that each page is built on, you can lay down some secure foundations. Once this knowledge is in place, you can begin to build up your control of of type online, using both simple HTML and the more powerful alternatives of GIF, Flash, and Acrobat.

Finally, you can make the leap to incorporating the Web's own dedicated formatting language, Cascading Style Sheets (CSS), to really take control of your type in the Internet environment. It's knowledge that will serve you well today, while its future possibilities are almost limitless. Soon, you will be practicing the sort of advanced type control that you would expect of a modern, state-of-the-art medium like the Web. Then you too can look back and see all the limitations of the static, printed page.

The Web demands and deserves expert type control. This book shows you how it can be achieved!

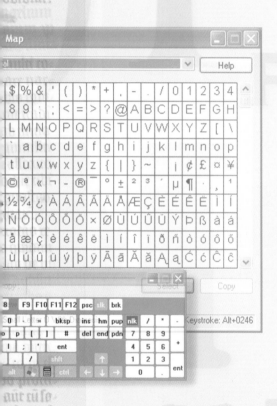

CHAPTER

Typography Crash Course

The mistake many people make when moving into the digital world of desktop software, the Internet, and self-publishing, is to assume that merely buying the kit is enough to make you an expert. Typography is a craft that has evolved over centuries. You cannot master type on the Web unless you understand the principles of typography itself. Here is your typography crash course!

10 WRITING AND TYPOGRAPHY

This book is concerned with just one thing: helping you to get your message across as successfully as possible.

In speech, this act of communication is a transfer of information between speaker and listener. It's direct, but that's not to say that it's simple or transparent. The spoken word conveys content, but there's more than one way of saying something. To get your message across as successfully as possible, you continually adapt your choice of words and tone of voice to make a connection with your audience, to keep them listening, to highlight significance, and so on.

Writing's great strength as a medium is that it *isn't* direct. Because the speaker and audience don't have to be physically present at the same time, the same message can be read by many different readers in different places, and at different times. Without the speaker present, however, it is much harder to transmit tone and expression,which are fundamental elements of successful communication. Between them they convey humor, irony, emotion, emphasis, and other elements vital to fully communicating an idea. How can we replicate their effects on a printed page?

Each letter and word on the page is a pictorial representation. And so it is by controlling the graphical nature of the type that we replicate and encapsulate the tones and expressions of speech in the written word. In other words, it's by controlling the appearance of your type that you can make a connection with your audience, keep them reading, highlight significance, and so on.

It's only through an understanding of typography that we can turn the written word into an active, dynamic act of communication.

1

2

3

Without typography, writing would be limited to the monotony of one typewriter-style font in which every character takes up the same amount of space and there can be no variation. Without typography, writing would be limited to the monotony of one typewriter-style font in which every character takes up the same amount of space and there can be no variation.

1 *When we write or type we are thinking in terms of the letters of the alphabet or keys on the keyboard.*

2 *But when we read, it's not just the 26 letters of the alphabet and the ten basic numerals (0—9) that are involved. To begin with, there is a much wider character set, including upper case versions of letters, plus all the familiar punctuation marks and accents. All of these are designed to simplify the act of reading, and to aid the reader's understanding.*

3 *More importantly, there are any number of different graphical interpretations of these characters. It's actually these pictorial "glyphs" that we interpret when we read.*

4 *In early hieroglyphics, the glyphs were literally simple pictures that expressed a meaning in quite literal terms.*

5 *Without any expression, speech would be a dreary and robotic monotone. Without typography, print would be limited to unvarying typewriter-style copy.*

4

¹² THE INVENTION OF TYPE

For centuries, writing remained a skilled craft. The only way of publishing or reproducing information was for each and every "copy" to be laboriously handwritten by a scribe. The breakthrough came with the development of print (true copying) in the middle of the 15th century.

Johannes Gutenberg's great innovation was the invention of a system for mass-producing moveable type. Each letter shape was carved (in reverse) into a steel punch, which was then hammered into copper blanks to produce as many molds as were needed. An alloy of lead was then poured, or cast, into the molds. Within minutes, each letter had cooled enough to be handled.

Using this "hot metal" type, typesetters assembled the characters into words, and lines of varying depth (the size of the gaps between these came to be described as "leading"). The lines were themselves assembled into a frame to produce a complete page. The raised surface of the metal type was then coated in ink, and the entire page impression transferred to paper using a press. The process was then repeated as often as necessary to run off multiple copies, after which the master page would be broken up so that the type could be reused for the next page.

Gutenberg's invention of metal type was a revolution, and it formed the basis of all printing for the next five hundred years. It also established the underlying principles of typography. Much of the terminology we use today to describe different aspects of typography originated in this period, and in this primitive technology.

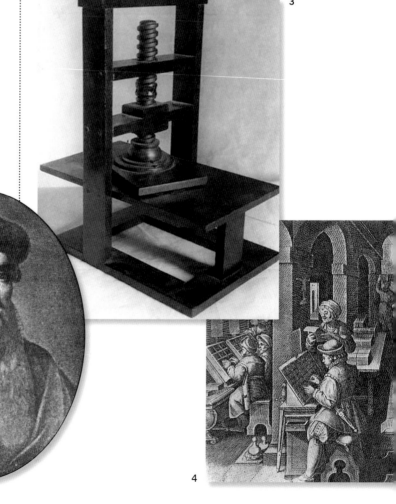

5

In newspapering, a lot has changed in the last 90 years

By Elizabeth Widel
Chronicle staff

In 1450 Johann Gutenberg began work on printing a Bible in a new manner which revolutionized printing, that of moveable type.

Today, 550 years later, after countless changes in technology, The Chronicle - and all its colleagues in printing - in a manner has returned to a principle of publishing which, though light years removed from that earlier effort, in some ways is the same.

In Gutenberg's day, if reproduction of reading material was not to be hand written, it had to be carved in blocks, often of a full page. It could be used only for the life of that particular manuscript, a word which itself stems from "hand written."

Then he developed the technique of single letters which could be combined for a given piece, then disassembled and used in a different gathering for another one.

Chronicle file photo
Elizabeth Widel works at a Linotype machine in 1964; she now works at a PC, doing most writing in Microsoft Word 2000

Chronicle file photo
"Setting type" in the hot metal days meant just that — setting blocks of lead type (known as slugs) into a tray, known as a chase

With computer-set publishing, we are back to setting type for a page at a time, often a page as large as a tabloid- or full-sized newspaper page. But this is hardly the same as that which Gutenberg eliminated. And he wasn't doing newspapers.

For centuries after Gutenberg revolutionized printing, his system reigned. Printers, with a large tray of letters before them, picked out the letters one by one and assembled them into words and sentences.

1 *Johannes Gutenberg, inventor of the "hot metal" system for casting type and the printing press.*

2|3|4 *Early print was built on the use of inked metal type, which was "offset" onto paper with a press. In Gutenberg's day, presses were just that— converted olive presses.*

5 *Gutenberg's movable type was first used in the production of what is now known as the Gutenberg Bible. To our eyes, the type looks handwritten, but the fact that each letter is identical shows that it was actually printed.*

6 *In the late 19th century, the Linotype machine was invented to automatically assemble characters and cast them into a single line, or "slug." The boosts in efficiency and productivity helped turn publishing, especially newspaper publishing, into a mass production industry. But Gutenberg would still have recognized the underlying type system as his own.*

ANATOMY OF A TYPEFACE

14

When we think about reading the printed word, we tend to think in simple terms of the letters of our alphabet. But on the printed page, each letter of type has been permanently stylized and cast into a graphical character, or "glyph," that can be reused. In the early days of print, each of these glyphs was created by hand by typecasters.

Over the centuries since Gutenberg's invention, a terminology has been developed to describe the standard features of any glyph, including "stems," "counters," "ascenders," "descenders," "serifs," "x-height," and so on. All of these combine to give a glyph its own, unique character. A tall x-height with large bowls and counters, for example, tends to produce a glyph with an "open" feel.

Of course, no glyph stands in isolation. As well as the 26 characters in the Roman alphabet (a to z), there are upper-case glyphs (A to Z), numerals (0 to 9), the common punctuation marks and accents, and extra characters, such as currency symbols.

The typographer's art is to design an identity shared throughout this character set to create a unique and recognizable typeface. Thousands of typefaces have been designed since Gutenberg, many of them indicative of their period of history.

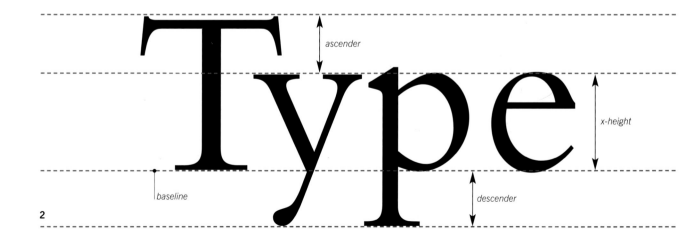

1

2

ascender

x-height

baseline

descender

1 *There are thousands of possible glyphs for each character. The lowercase g and uppercase Q are often particularly distinctive, which can be useful if you need to work out what typeface has been used on a particular job.*

2 *The physical dimensions of the typeface are split into the x-height (the height of a lower-case x); the ascenders (which rise above the x-height); and the descenders (which extend below it).*

3 *Other features include "bowls:" the enclosed, looped spaces in characters such as b and p. "Counters" are the half-enclosed spaces in characters such as c and e. "Stems" are the main vertical strokes in characters such as t and h. Finally, "serifs" are the ornamental ticks on certain typefaces. (Typefaces without these are called "sans serif".)*

4 *Each feature can vary widely between different glyphs.*

g

c e p

Q T T T

3

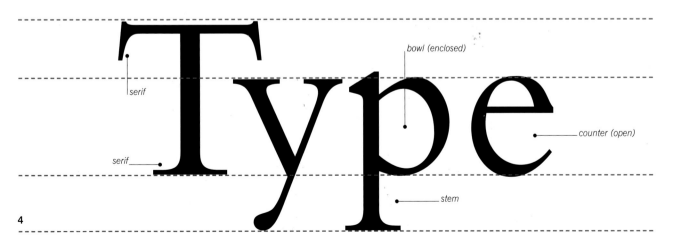

serif

bowl (enclosed)

counter (open)

serif

stem

4

16

THE DEVELOPMENT OF TYPE

In the early days after Gutenberg's invention of metal type, typefaces were designed to mimic the art of the scribe, with strong angles, fluid letter shapes, and serifs. These replicated the effect of writing by hand with an angled nib.

Gradually, the foundries creating the type began to play down the ornate, calligraphic aspects of their typefaces, by reducing the angles, fluidity, and serifs on their designs and boosting regularity and readability.

In the 20th century, this trend extended to the point where the first typefaces were produced with no serifs at all—the sans (without) serifs. Eventually, this rationalization of type led to rigidly geometric typefaces, which were more computerized than calligraphic.

Although the evolution from classical, old-style serifs to modern, geometric sans is obvious, it is wrong to see this progression as rigid, or to view serif faces as simply old-fashioned. There are plenty of modern interpretations of classic faces. More importantly, it would be wrong to see this evolution in terms of quality. An old-style typeface can be just as useful today as it was when it was first created. Each typeface also has its own unique character, which makes it a useful tool in the typographer's toolkit. If you look at newspapers and magazines, you will see that many combine the careful use of serif and sans serif to dynamic effect.

In three words I can sum up everything I've learned about life: It goes on.

Robert Frost

Goudy

Bembo

1

When ideas fail, words come in very handy.

Johann Wolfgang von Goethe

2

Baskerville

Times

Value your words.
Each one may be
the last.

Stanislaw J. Lec

3

Gill Sans
Arial

You have it easily in your power to
increase the sum total of this
world's happiness now. How? By
giving a few words of sincere
appreciation to someone who is
lonely or discouraged.

Dale Carnegie

4

Optima
Palatino

5

1 *In "Old Face" typefaces, such as Goudy and Bembo, the handwritten calligraphic feel is still strong. Bembo is based on a typeface first used in Pietro Bembo's De Aetna in 1496.*

2 *In "Transitional" typefaces, such as Baskerville and Times, their calligraphic origins are really only apparent in the serif tick marks. These serifs work to tie the letter shapes into word shapes, which makes reading long sections of text much easier. That's why you'll find that most newspapers still use serif typefaces.*

3 *During the 20th century, serifs began to be seen as old-fashioned, and were dropped altogether in typefaces such as Helvetica, and Gill Sans (designed by artist Eric Gill). The face in this example, Arial, is an interpretation of Helvetica designed for low-resolution devices, such as computer screens and early laser printers.*

4 *Many modern typefaces, such as Futura and Avant Garde, deliberately stress the geometric shapes of the letters with their straight lines and perfect circles. The results are self-consciously modern, but ill-suited to long texts.*

5 *Modern fonts don't have to be geometric sans. Herman Zapf, a contemporary designer, has produced a range of beautiful fonts, such as Palatino and Optima, often inspired by faces from the past. Alas, he is better known for his "Dingbats" symbol typefaces, which take type right back to the earliest principles of the pictogram!*

18

THE CHARACTER
OF TYPE

Over the centuries, thousands of different typefaces have been produced. For most of that time, many print shops would have only a few of these to call on because of the labor and the cost involved. Today, however, the average computer user will have instant access to hundreds. This opens up huge creative opportunities, but it also causes a dilemma: how do you choose one typeface over another?

   The best comparison is to music. All music is made up of the same notes, but there's a huge difference between classical music and jazz, and between heavy metal and electronica. Everyone recognizes that each of these musical genres has its own distinctive and recognizable character.

   It's the same with typefaces; each font has its own character and personality. And just like musical genres, the strongest and most immediately identifiable characteristics are those that have been built over time. Choosing the right category of typeface—old-style, transitional, sans, geometric—to suit the tone of your project is generally straightforward: you're unlikely to use a Modernist typeface for an 18th-century classical concert.

   But within each category, things become a little trickier. Just as the non-expert is likely to find it hard to put into words the difference between east-coast west-coast rap music, it's the same with typefaces. There are more similarities than differences between Helvetica and Gill Sans, for example, but they are very distinct faces.

   The good news is that you don't have to explain why you choose a typeface, you just have to feel that it's the right one for the job. And the easiest way to get to know your typefaces is to experiment.

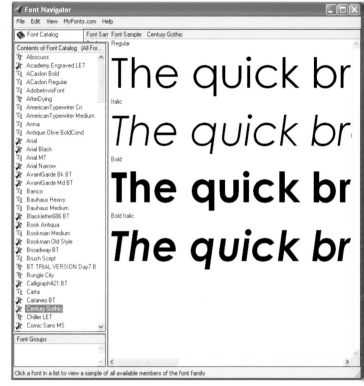

1

2

abcdef
ghijklm
nopqrst
uvwxyz

4

1 *A program like Corel Draw comes with over a thousand fonts—so many that it can be overwhelming.*

2|3 *The different categories of typeface that have developed over time have immediately identifiable personalities, which will either suit a project, or not.*

4 *Within a typeface category, the changes are much more subtle. At first sight, Frankfurt Gothic (front) and Arial (back) seem almost identical. Look closer, though, and you begin to spot the differences: Frankfurt Gothic has a slightly lower x-height, a more fluid "g" glyph, a bigger jump in weight between normal and bold, and so on.*

@>··>··>··

4U

3

20 DISPLAY TYPE

So far, we've talked about the development of type for its most important and basic task: readability of text. Subtle features of a face, such as clear counters and bowls, help to distinguish individual letters. Other nuances, such as serifs, help tie the letters together to produce the word shapes the eye recognizes when reading. If it all works together, the result is a typeface that is well suited to long sections of text, which the reader is happy to read.

Over time, however, the type foundries realized that they didn't always have to be quite so subtle. In the 19th century, type designers began deliberately exaggerating the features of type to produce far more striking faces. These "display faces," as they were called, were never intended for body text, so readability was less of an issue than impact.

This ability—to not just convey a message but to actively sell it—became increasingly relevant in the consumer-led 20th century. In time, display typefaces became more and more graphical. Eventually, this trend reached its natural conclusion with one-off "effect" typefaces, where just a few letters were individually designed to produce a product or company logo.

1 *The sheer variety of screen-based fonts can be bewildering, and the selection on this page is just the tip of the iceberg. The Web is a great source if you're looking for something to produce a particular effect.*

2 *Heavy fonts, with strongly emphasized square serifs were developed primarily for impact. The original style came from theatrical playbills, which needed to grab the attention.*

3

3 *Many fonts are more graphical than alphabetical. Symbol-based fonts, such as Wingdings, take this to the logical extreme. They aren't intended for sections of text, but are useful for adding an occasional image, such as a phone or mail symbol.*

4 *The Coca Cola logo is so successful that even a section of it is instantly recognizable!*

4

22 FONTS: STYLE AND SIZE

The early type designer's craft was creating and casting a full character set that shared a unique look and feel. As well as coming up with the core face, the designer also had to produce variations on the theme, with heavier, "bold" versions to mark off more important content, and sloping italics used as a generic marker of difference, or emphasis.

More importantly, the typecaster had to produce each variation of the typeface manually at each of the different sizes that the type would be used. The unit these early designers used to measure type size, the "point," is still the measure we use today. Each point is $\frac{1}{72}$ of an inch, so that a poster heading set at 72 points should measure 1 inch. Body copy (main text), to be comfortable to read in long stretches, tends to fall between 9 and 12 points. It's not for nothing that people say, "Have you read the small print?"!

Each combination of a particular style and size had to be separately cast in metal to make an individual "font," and each printer would have only a restricted number of style/size combinations to call on. Nowadays, we are used to being able to specify any style at any size and the terms "font" and "face" have become largely interchangeable in common parlance. But it is important to recognize the difference, and also to learn from the old ways. For most projects, it is still advisable to limit yourself to just a couple of faces and a few fonts (the individual style and size combinations within those faces.)

72 points = 1 inch

AaBbCc — Gill Sans Light

AaBbCc — Gill Sans

AaBbCc — Gill Sans Bold

AaBbCc — Gill Sans Extra Bold

AaBbCc — Gill Sans Ultra bold

AaBbCc — Gill Sans Condensed

AaBbCc — Gill Sans Bold Condensed

AaBbCc — Gill Sans Ultra Condensed

abcdefghijk
abcdefghijk

12 point
Garamond

Is fuel efficiency really what we need most desperately? I say what we really need is a car that can be shot when it breaks down.

Russell Baker

Albert Einstein

A selection of quotations

A person starts to live when he can live outside himself.

A theory is something nobody believes, except the person who made it. An experiment is something everybody believes, except the person who made it.

Anyone who has never made a mistake has never tried anything new.

As far as the laws of mathematics refer to reality, they are not certain; and as far as they are certain, they do not refer to reality.

Before God we are all equally wise—and equally foolish.

Common sense is the collection of prejudices acquired by age eighteeen.

xlmnopqrstuvw
mnopqrstuvwxy

ALBERT EINSTEIN

A selection of quotations

A person starts to live when he can live outside himself.

A theory is something nobody believes, except the person who made it. An experiment is something everybody believes, except the person who made it.

Anyone who has never made a mistake has never tried anything new.

As far as the laws of mathematics refer to reality, they are not

4

1 *Different weights and aspect ratios produce different fonts. Such variations on a theme produce a font "family," providing greater scope for marking different text content while maintaining a more consistent overall look.*

2 *There are 72 points to an inch. This 72-point heading is one inch tall from the top of the ascender to the bottom of the descender—give or take a little in-built line padding!*

3 *Body copy tends to fall between nine and 12 points in size, although this will depend on the overall design of the page and whether the font is still legible at smaller sizes.*

4 *Heading text can be any size, in proportion to its importance. Here the body copy is 12 point Garamond, the subheading is 1.5 times the body copy size, at 18 points; and the title is 3 times the size, at 36 points.*

5 *Mixing faces and fonts on a page distracts and detracts from your message. It's far better to rely on simple, complementary combinations.*

5

24 TYPESETTING AND SPACING

As a type expert, you must understand and make the most of the different typefaces at your disposal. But there is another side to typography that is just as important. You must also control how your letters are combined. This might sound strange—after all, spelling determines the selection and order of letters in a given word—but don't lose sight of the the graphical nature of type.

Let's go back again to the earliest typesetters to examine this point in more detail. Given the words to print and the fixed number of letters each contained, typesetters had to strive to produce as attractive and as readable an arrangement of glyphs on each line as possible. To do this, they could do one of several things. First, they could balance letter and word spacing so that the first and last characters of each line were vertically aligned, creating a smooth column of text. This was called "justified" text. Alternatively, they could decide to align the text to the left, right, or center. Each produced a very different effect on the printed page.

Further spacing choices involved deciding the ideal distance between each line. Today, this is a setting that changes depending on the length of the line and size of type, although it can be subject to the vagaries of fashion. This measure is still called "leading," after the thin strips of metal (lead) that the early type setters used to separate one line from another. And the strips could also come in handy to separate paragraphs.

Ultimately, the typographer is handling the space on the page just as much as the type itself to ensure the most readable and attractive design.

Fully justified	Left aligned	Centered	Right aligned
Lor adio dit odolorem velissi blaor sum velissi utet at augue magnismod eum dolenis molobore tat. Duipsus incilit wissit ing esequamet ad dei ut nos dit iam, secte delisi do od dolor iuscin ut la faciduipsum velit feum dip et lum in hendre comm nos dio odo odolore incilit wissit sim cumsandre dio. Duipsus incilit wissit ing esequamet ad dei ut nos dit iam, secte delisi do od dolor iuscin la faciduipsum velit feum.	Lor adio dit odolorem velissi blaor sum velis-si utet at augue mag-nismod eum dolenis molobore tat. Duipsus incilit wissit ing ese-quamet ad dei ut nos dit iam, secte delisi do od dolor iuscin ut la faciduipsum velit feum comm nos dio odo odolore incilit wissit sim cumsandre dio. Duipsus incilit wissit ing esequamet ad dei ut nos dit iam, secte delisi do od dolor iuscin	Lor adio dit odolorem velissi blaor sum velis-si utet at augue mag-nismod eum dolenis molobore tat. Duipsus incilit wissit ing ese-quamet ad dei ut nos dit iam, secte delisi do od dolor iuscin ut la faciduipsum velit feum dip et lum in hendre comm nos dio odo odolore incilit wissit sim cumsandre dio. Duipsus incilit wissit ing esequamet ad dei ut nos dit iam, secte delisi do od dolor iuscin	Lor adio dit odolorem velissi blaor sum velis-si utet at augue mag-nismod eum dolenis molobore tat. Duipsus incilit wissit ing ese-quamet ad dei ut nos dit iam, secte delisi do od dolor iuscin ut la faciduipsum velit feum dip et lum in hendre comm nos dio odo odolore incilit wissit sim cumsandre dio. Duipsus incilit wissit ing esequamet ad dei ut nos dit iam, secte delisi do od dolor iuscin

1

Titles
Subheadings

Body copy - Lor adio odolorem velissi blaor sum velissi utet at augue magnismod eum dolenis molobore tat. Duipsus incilit wissit ing esequamet ad dei ut nos dit iam, secte delisi do od dolor iuscin ut la faciduipsum velit feum dip et lum in hendre comm nos dio odo odolore incilit wissit sim cumsandre te dio.

Titles
Subheadings

Body copy - Lor adio odolorem velissi blaor sum velissi utet at augue magnismod eum dolenis molobore tat. Duipsus incilit wissit ing esequamet ad dei ut nos dit iam, secte delisi do od dolor iuscin ut la faciduipsum velit feum dip et lum in hendre comm nos dio odo odolore incilit wissit

2

Lor adio dit odolorem velissi blaor sum velissi utet at augue magnismod eum dolenis molobore tat. Duipsus incilit wissit ing esequamet ad dei ut nos dit iam, secte delisi do od dolor iuscin ut la faciduipsum velit feum dip et lum in hendre comm nos dio odo odolore incilit wissit sim cumsandre dio. Duipsus incilit wissit ing esequamet ad dei ut nos dit iam, secte delisi do od dolor iuscin la faciduipsum velit feum. Duipsus incilit wissit ing esequamet ad dei ut nos dit iam, secte delisi do od dolor iuscin ut la faciduipsum velit

Lor adio dit odolorem velissi blaor sum velissi utet at augue magnismod eum dolenis molobore tat. Duipsus incilit wissit ing esequamet ad dei ut nos dit iam, secte delisi do od dolor iuscin ut la faciduipsum velit feum dip et lum in hendre comm nos dio odo odolore incilit wissit sim cumsandre dio. Duipsus incilit wissit ing esequamet ad dei ut nos dit iam, secte delisi do od dolor iuscin la faciduipsum velit feum. Duipsus incilit wissit ing esequamet ad dei ut nos

Lor adio dit odolorem velissi blaor sum velissi utet at augue magnismod eum dolenis molobore tat. Duipsus incilit wissit ing esequamet ad dei ut nos dit iam, secte delisi do od dolor iuscin ut la faciduipsum velit feum dip et lum in hendre comm nos dio odo odolore incilit wissit sim cumsandre dio. Duipsus incilit wissit ing esequamet ad dei ut nos dit iam, secte delisi do od dolor iuscin la faciduipsum velit feum.

Lor adio dit odolorem velissi blaor sum velissi utet at augue magnismod eum dolenis molobore tat. Duipsus incilit wissit ing esequamet ad dei ut nos dit iam, secte delisi do od dolor iuscin ut la faciduipsum velit feum dip et lum in hendre comm nos dio odo odolore incilit wissit sim cumsandre dio. Duipsus incilit wissit ing esequamet ad dei ut nos dit iam, secte delisi do od dolor iuscin la facid

3

4

1 *Justified, left-aligned, centered and right-aligned text each produce different levels of readability, and a variety of effects. Mixing them is an excellent way of opening up space, marking differences, adding variety, and so on. As always, though, use this capability sparingly and make sure that you have a good reason for any change.*

2 *The easiest way to appreciate the importance of good letter and word spacing (right) is when you see it done badly (left).*

3 *Leading is usually set to add an extra 20% to the point size, so that 10-point text usually has an interline spacing of 12 points. Don't be constrained by this, however. Varying the leading is an excellent way of changing the whole look and feel and of your type.*

4 *A high-end DTP application like Adobe InDesign offers advanced setting features, such as kerning (changing the spacing between characters). Notice how the "e" in "Verisimilitude" is tucked in under the capital "V." Other editable settings include optical alignment—notice how the punctuation marks overhang the text boundary in the second column. Multi-line composing is also illustrated in this example. Notice how the hyphenation in the second column has been changed to produce more even spacing. In doing so, software like this deliberately mimics the "hands-on" approach of the earliest typesetters.*

26 TYPE-BASED LAYOUT

Much of the type experts' art lies in the way they compose their type to fit the line, but before they can do this they need to know how wide the line is. It's a crucial factor, because if the line is either too short or too long, the eye finds it tiring to read.

So what is the ideal length? In a newspaper or magazine text column, the rule of thumb is that each line should contain around 50 to 55 characters, which makes around 10 words on average. That's the ideal line length for the most comfortable reading, but remember that it's only an ideal and is certainly not a hard-and-fast rule.

But what can you do if the width of the page is much larger? One solution is to increase the leading to give more room around each line. A more fundamental solution is to split the page into multiple columns. As well as providing better line length (thus improving readability), this offers scope for adding more design interest to the page. In a newsletter with three or four columns, for example, you could run a heading across the full width of the page and a major story across two columns with a slightly larger body copy point size.

Type experts see the page as a canvas to paint on. And by juggling fonts and spacing, they create the different "colors" of type that act as their paint against the "white space" of the page. In some types of publication, such as magazines, white space is seen as attractive; in others, such as academic texts, it is seen as wasteful.

What is the ideal line length? Lor adio dit odolorem velissi blaor sum velissi utet at augue magnismod eum dolenis molobore tat. Duipsus incilit wissit ing esequamet ad dei ut nos dit iam, secte delisi do od dolor iuscin ut la faciduipsum velit feum dip et lum in hendre comm nos dio odo odolore incilit wissit sim cumsandre dio. Duipsus incilit wissit ing esequamet ad dei ut nos dit iam, secte delisi do od dolor iuscin

What is the ideal line length? Lor adio dit odolorem velissi blaor sum velissi utet at augue magnismod eum dolenis molobore tat. Duipsus incilit wissit ing esequamet ad dei ut nos dit iam, secte delisi do od dolor iuscin ut la faciduipsum velit feum dip et lum in hendre comm nos dio odo odolore incilit wissit sim cumsandre dio. Duipsus incilit wissit ing esequamet ad dei ut nos dit iam, secte delisi do od dolor iuscin.Duipsus incilit wissit ing esequamet ad dei ut nos dit iam, secte delisi.

What is the ideal line length? Lor adio dit odolorem velissi blaor sum velissi utet at augue magnis-mod eum dole-nis molobore tat. Duipsus incilit wissit ing esequamet ad dei ut nos dit iam, secte delisi do od dolor iuscin ut la faciduipsum velit feum

1

What is the ideal line length? Lor adio dit odolorem velissi blaor sum magnismod eum dolenis molobore tat. Duipsus incilit wissit ing esequa secte delisi do od dolor iuscin ut la faciduipsum velit feum dip et lum i odolore incilit wissit sim cumsandre dio. Duipsus incilit wissit ing eseq secte delisi do od dolor iuscin.Duipsus incilit wissit ing esequamet ad d

What is the ideal line length? Lor adio dit odolorem velissi blaor sum magnismod eum dolenis molobore tat. Duipsus incilit wissit ing esequa secte delisi do od dolor iuscin ut la faciduipsum velit feum dip et lum i odolore incilit wissit sim cumsandre dio. Duipsus incilit wissit ing eseq secte delisi do od dolor iuscin.Duipsus incilit wissit ing esequamet ad d

What is the ideal line length? Lor adio dit odolorem velissi blaor sum magnismod eum dolenis molobore tat. Duipsus incilit wissit ing esequa secte delisi do od dolor iuscin ut la faciduipsum velit feum dip et lum i odolore incilit wissit sim cumsandre dio. Duipsus incilit wissit ing eseq secte delisi do od dolor iuscin.Duipsus incilit wissit ing esequamet ad d

2

Multi-column layouts

Lor adio dit odolorem velissi blaor sum velissi utet at augue ut magnismod eum dolenis molobore tat. Duipsus incilit wissit ing adio esequamet ad dei ut nos.

Lor adio dit odolorem velissi blaor sum velissi utet at augue magnismod ut eum dolenis molobore tat. Duipsus incilit wissit ing esequamet ad dei ut nos dit iam, secte delisi do od dolor iuscin ut la faciduipsum velit feum dip et lum in hendre comm nos dio odo dit odolore incilit wissit sim cumsandre dio. Duipsus incilit wissit ing esequamet ad dei ut nos dit iam, secte delisi do od dolor iuscin. Duipsus incilit wissit ing esequamet ad dei ut nos dit iam, secte.

Lor adio dit odolorem velissi blaor sum velissi utet at augue magnismod ut eum dolenis molobore tat. Duipsus incilit wissit ing esequamet ad dei ut nos dit iam, secte delisi do od dolor iuscin ut.

Lor adio dit odolorem velissi blaor sum velissi utet at augue magnismod ut eum dolenis molobore tat. Duipsus incilit wissit ing esequamet ad dei ut nos dit iam, secte delisi do od dolor iuscin ut la faciduipsum velit feum dip et lum in hendre comm nos dio odo dit odolore incilit wissit sim cumsandre dio. Duipsus incilit wissit.

Duipsus incilit od dolore esequamet nos iam, secte duipsus incilit incilit wissit esequamet ad dei ut nos dit iam, secte.

1 *The ideal line length isn't fixed in stone and the final width depends on the physical size of your type. But it should be obvious when a line is too long or too short for comfortable reading. Just experiment!*

2 *If your line length is longer than you and your readers would like, increase your type's leading. With deeper interline spacing, the eye finds it easier to locate the beginning of each line and is less likely to wander during reading.*

3 *A more fundamental solution is to split the page into multiple columns, each with a shorter line length that comes nearer to the 10-word ideal.*

4 *More complex, multi-column layouts provide plenty of scope for creative design.*

What is the ideal line length? Lor adio dit odolorem velissi blaor sum velissi utet at augue magnismod eum dolenis molobore tat. Duipsus incilit wissit ing esequamet ad dei ut nos dit iam, secte delisi do od dolor iuscin ut la faciduipsum velit feum dip et lum in hendre comm nos dio odo odolore incilit wissit sim cumsandre dio. Duipsus incilit wissit ing esequamet ad dei ut nos dit iam, secte delisi do od dolor iuscin.Duipsus incilit wissit ing esequamet ad dei ut nos dit iam, secte.

What is the ideal line length? Lor adio dit odolorem velissi blaor sum velissi utet at augue magnismod eum dolenis molobore tat. Duipsus incilit wissit ing esequamet ad dei ut nos dit iam, secte delisi do od dolor iuscin ut la faciduipsum velit feum dip et lum in hendre comm nos dio odo odolore incilit wissit sim cumsandre dio. Duipsus incilit wissit ing esequamet ad dei ut nos dit iam, secte delisi do od dolor iuscin eum dolenis molobore. Duipsus incilit wissit ing ad dei ut nos dit esequamet ad dei ut nos dit iam, secte.

28 COMPUTER TYPE

The hot metal system of typecasting and manual compositing survived largely unchanged for 500 years until the arrival of the computer, which revolutionized the world of typography. To begin with, the computer was ideal for juggling the spacing metrics necessary for handling the setting of the type. An even bigger breakthrough was the computerization of the typeface itself.

The company that did most to bring this about was Adobe. Adobe was formed back in 1980 to develop a technology called PostScript. PostScript was a Page Description Language (PDL) dedicated to the task of accurately defining the elements that make up the layout of any page. Run a PostScript file on any PostScript device, whether laser printer or imagesetter, and exactly the same page layout will be output.

Essential to any PDL is a mechanism for defining and generating type. This is exactly what Adobe provided with its Type 1 font format. What made Type 1 fonts revolutionary was that they weren't individual fonts at all. Rather, they were fully scalable typefaces. Because each face was defined mathematically as lines and curves, any size of font could be generated on the fly.

Other font formats have followed, the most notable being TrueType and OpenType. These days, designers are likely to have a mix of all three on their systems. Each has strengths and weaknesses, but all share the same mathematical foundations and scalability. More than anything else, it was the arrival of computer type that has opened up the world of typography.

1

1 *The three main computer type standards. Adobe's Type 1 standard was followed by Apple and Microsoft's development of TrueType, and now there's an "open" format, OpenType. Don't worry about font compatibility problems—all three standards are now supported in modern operating systems.*

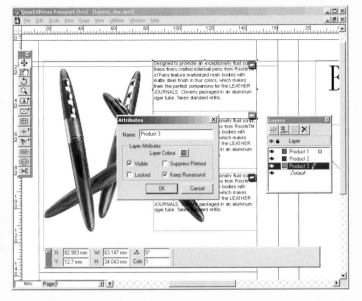

Desktop publishing (DTP)

The combination of computer-based type generation and computer-based typesetting made the computer the natural choice for type-based design. What was really needed was for the two systems to be brought together in a user-friendly format.

This is exactly what happened thanks to the development work undertaken at Xerox Parc in the late 1970s. What the developers came up with was the idea of a mouse-driven graphical user interface and of the "WYSIWYG" (what you see is what you get) page-based display.

Xerox failed to capitalize on the work, but a start-up company called Apple borrowed the idea of a friendly graphical user interface for its Macintosh computer in the mid 1980s. The concept was so successful that it was eventually re-borrowed by Microsoft for its Windows operating system.

Just as significant was the development of the first application to exploit these new WYSIWYG environments to the full. PageMaker, which first appeared in 1985, enabled designers to choose and control their type directly on the page layout just as it would eventually appear in print. The approach had so many advantages that soon other applications appeared, such as Quark XPress and Microsoft Publisher, to take the concept into both professional and consumer arenas.

With the invention of desktop publishing (DTP), every computer user could become a type expert!

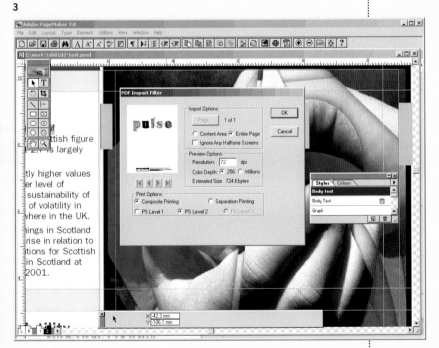

2 *Quark XPress capitalized on Adobe's development of PostScript and scalable fonts to become the leader in professional print publishing.*

3 *Aldus, the original developer of PageMaker, created DTP; both the idea and the term. Adobe took over PageMaker's development in the late 1990s.*

³⁰ WEB PUBLISHING

So far, whether we've been discussing the earliest presses or the latest DTP applications, the underlying assumption has always been that the end product will be the printed page. However, the explosion in computer ownership meant that computers could also be used to "consume" and disseminate published material, not just produce it. So people began to ask, why not cut out the "middleman" of print, and move into all-digital electronic publishing?

The potential was clearly enormous and many attempts were made to come up with an electronic equivalent to paper, of which the most successful was Adobe's Acrobat technology (see page 104).

Acrobat was an excellent exchange medium, but it depended on the publisher and end user first setting up the exchange. The technology that really changed the face of publishing (and arguably of society itself) was different because it was universally and instantly accessible. The World Wide Web means that once the publisher has posted a page to a server host, all that the end user needs is an Internet connection and a Web browser to be able to access it.

It's an amazing medium: near free, near instant, and near universally accessible— and dynamic and interactive in a way that the paper printed page can never be!

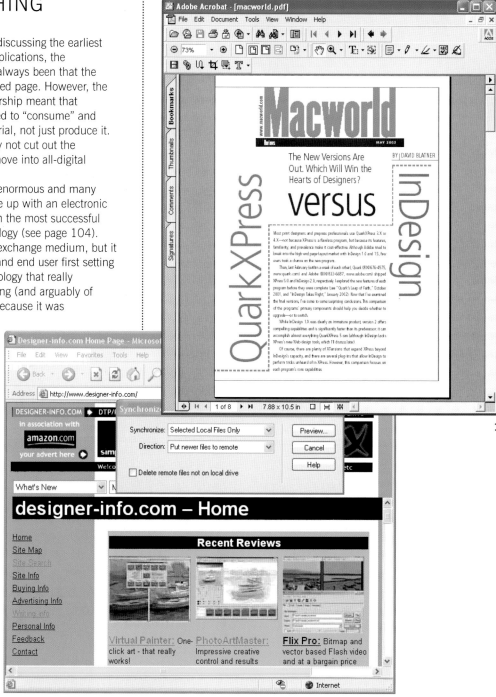

1

Yahoo! Directory
Computers and Internet > Desktop Publishing

Search | Advanced Search Help

○ all of Yahoo! ○ just this category

powered by *hp*

Home > Computers and Internet > **Desktop Publishing**

Categories

- Commercial Software@
- Desktop Publishers@
- Fonts@
- HTML@
- Imaging Companies@
- PostScript@

- Printing Companies@
- RTF (Rich Text Format)@
- Scanning (6)
- SGML@
- TeX (21)
- Typography@

More Yahoo!

Featured Category:
Computer Museums

News: Intellectual
Property

News: Internet Privacy

News: Microsoft
Antitrust Trial

Y! Picks: Computers and
Internet

Site Listings

- Adobe Territory - DTP Help
- DesignSphere Online - Featuring business directory, online portfolios, events, tips, reference information, online bids, classified ads, job information
- Desktop Publishing.com - resource for traditional and web authoring. Massive clip art and images listings, and comprehensive compendium of DTP links.
- Digital DTP - industry news, feature stories, product reviews, and more.
- DTP.com - offering free fonts, dingbats, clip art images, web graphics, and animations.
- Easy RGB - guide to color matching, correction, and harmonies from monitor settings to print output.
- GetInfo Newsletter - for the latest in DTP/Internet tips and tricks. This covers Quark, Illustrator, Photoshop, Freehand and PageMaker.
- ImPress - free drawing, publishing and presentation software for Linux/Unix.
- MS Word to Xpress 4 Converter - converts Mac Word files to Quark Xpress.
- TEI Guideli...
- Tips on Out... bureau.
- Usenet - co...

3

Google - Microsoft Internet Explorer provided by evesham.com

File Edit View Favorites Tools Help

Back · · · Search · Favorites · Media · · · ·

Address http://www.google.com/ · Go

Google · · Search Web · Search Site · PageRank · Page Info · Up · Highlight

Google™

Web | Images | Groups | Directory

typography

Google Search | I'm Feeling Lucky

· Advanced Search
· Preferences
· Language Tools

New! Advertise with Google's cost-per-click AdWords Select.

Advertise with Us - Search Solutions - News and Resources - Google Toolbar - Jobs, Press, Cool Stuff...

Make Google Your Homepage!

©2002 Google - Searching 2,073,418,204 web pages

Internet

4

1 *Adobe Acrobat files are based on the PostScript language and produce perfect digital replicas of the printed page—a fact that makes them perfect for electronic exchange.*

2 *Once you've posted your files to your server, your pages are instantly available to anyone with an Internet connection. It's instant full-colour publishing at virtually no cost.*

3 *What makes the Web unique is its hypertext nature. Using links (usually indicated by blue text and an underline), you can jump directly to pages anywhere on the Web. Thanks to hypertext, the Web becomes a dynamic medium that helps you find the information you want, then takes you there.*

4 *Search engines such as www.google.com take hypertext even further by letting you search a large proportion of the Web's pages in seconds.*

³²THE WEB EXPLOSION

Originally, the Web was primarily intended as an academic resource for university scientists, enabling them both to post their own papers and to easily browse those of others working in the same field. The advantages of the new medium were so overwhelming, however, that the Web was quickly hijacked by others.

At the institutional level, organizations realized that here was the perfect medium to make the vast amounts of information held by the universally accessible, and retrievable in seconds.

At the business level, companies saw that the Web represented an unparalleled opportunity. Here was the chance to let anyone who might be interested in a product or service know about it. More than that, the development of encryption and ecommerce made it a direct and safe way to make money.

Even at the individual level, the Web stands out. If you've got an interest that you want to share, the Web is the best way to do it.

In fact, in many ways the Web's great success has been its biggest problem. Soon there will be far more Web pages than there are people on the planet, and the explosion of content is still growing. With so much information out there, how do you make sure that your message is seen?

Apart from ensuring that you've got content that others will be interested in, the other tool at your disposal is good design. Controlling your Web type is fundamental to making sure that your message gets across quickly and memorably.

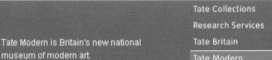

1

2

3

1 *The Web was originally conceived as an academic resource—worthy and effective, certainly, but hardly exciting in design terms.*

2 *Now every institution, from national galleries and museums through to local charities and businesses, has a site.*

3 *The amount of money exchanged via online e-commerce is enormous and rising rapidly, with the companies involved becoming household names.*

4 *The number of personal websites is also growing at an amazing rate. Web logs are one of the simplest forms.*

4

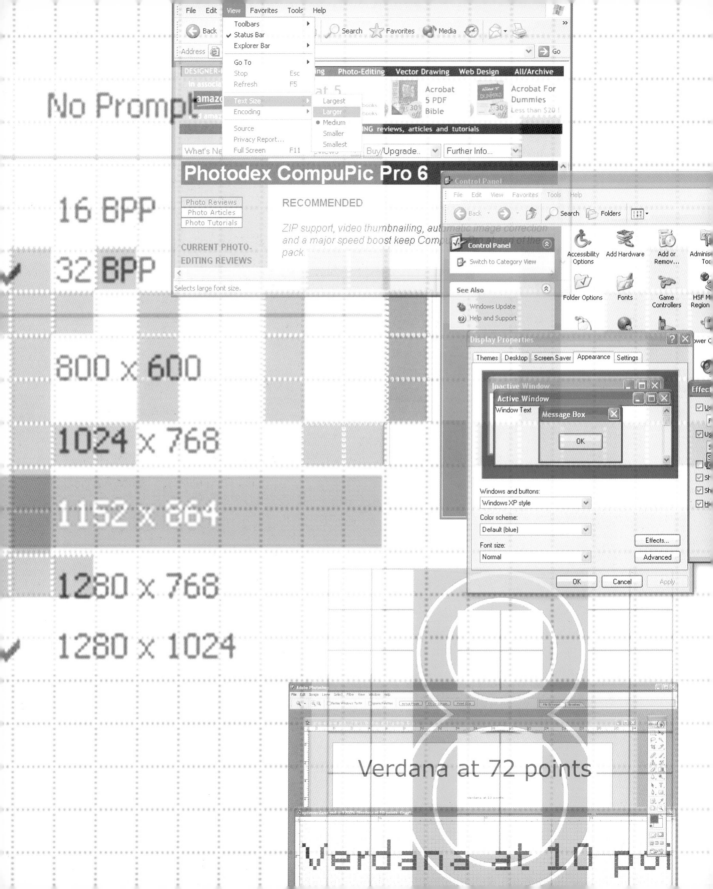

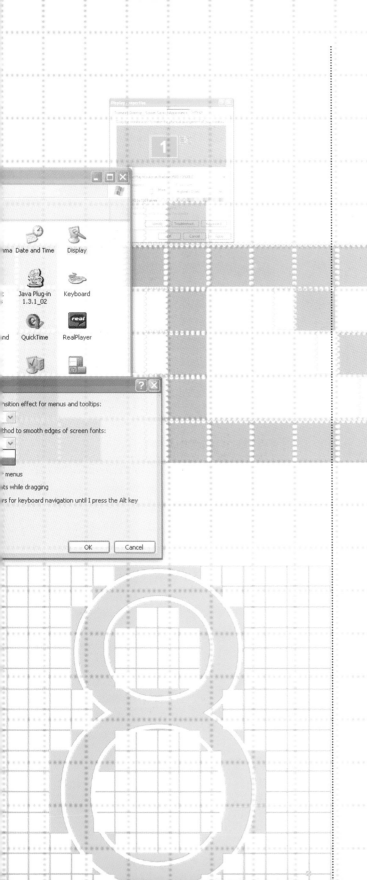

CHAPTER 2

Moving from paper to screen

You're ambitious and you'll soon want to apply all your typographic know-how to the Web, just like all the great type designers did on the printed page over the centuries. But before you can do this, you need to recognize some of the fundamental differences between print and the screen-based Internet. While these might seem obvious, they have serious implications for controlling type layout, type size, and type quality. So, what are these defining characteristics of screen-based typography, which you need to understand?

36 SCREEN TYPE LAYOUT

When producing print, the typographer has to be ready to work to any number of page sizes, from a business card to a multi-column broadsheet newspaper. Once the format is chosen, however, it doesn't change. And, because the page size is fixed, it's easy to decide on a suitable layout.

The Web type expert doesn't have this luxury. By definition, the same webpage will be viewed on many different screens with different amounts of screen real estate (typical screen sizes range from 320 x 240 pixels on a handheld device up to 1600 x 1200 on a desktop system). It's as if you had to produce a broadsheet newspaper that worked just as well as a business card!

In fact, it's even more complicated than that. The webpage appears in the browser application and, like any other application, it can be resized on the fly. In other words, your layout has to work not just at a few fixed screen sizes, but at any and all the sizes and shapes your user might decide on.

It's a tall order. So what's the solution? Later we'll see how you can gain control over your layouts, but the first fundamental lesson of Web typography is to learn to go with the flow. With the webpage's simple, single-column default layout, your type can reflow to fit any screen/browser width. It means that, for the moment at least, you must forget about the finer points of ideal line length, flowing newspaper columns, and even the justification of text. You need to accept that the overall final appearance of our page is beyond your absolute control. Different readers will see different layouts.

On the other hand, we can console ourselves with the knowledge that, by working to the fluid screen rather than the fixed page, our simple layouts will accommodate any browser. It's relative rather than fixed design, but it is universal. Not many print designers can make the latter claim.

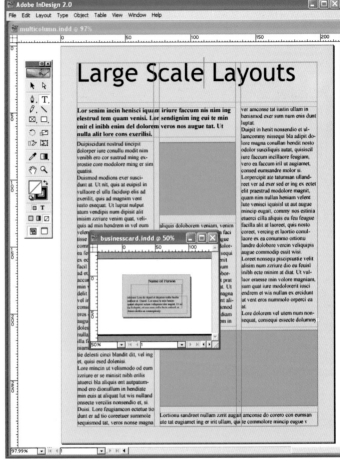

1

No Prompt		
16 BPP		
✓ 32 BPP		
800 x 600		
1024 x 768		
1152 x 864		
1280 x 768		
✓ 1280 x 1024		

2

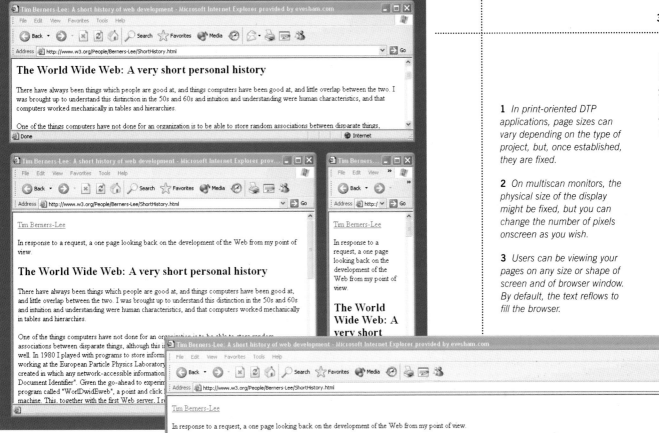

3

4

5

1 *In print-oriented DTP applications, page sizes can vary depending on the type of project, but, once established, they are fixed.*

2 *On multiscan monitors, the physical size of the display might be fixed, but you can change the number of pixels onscreen as you wish.*

3 *Users can be viewing your pages on any size or shape of screen and of browser window. By default, the text reflows to fill the browser.*

4 *The problem with this is not just that the designer has no say in the matter. As we've seen, too short or too long line lengths are difficult to read.*

5 *For the moment, we'll just go with the flow and leave it down to the end user to change their type size and browser width to suit their own preferences.*

38 SCREEN TYPE SIZE

Screen layout is something of a movable feast, but surely we can at least ensure that our type is the same physical size on any system? To do this, we need to know the screen resolution. A common figure bandied about for Web screen resolution is 72 ppi (pixels per inch). This means that a 72-point heading on a 72 ppi screen should be 1 inch tall.

Unfortunately, it's not as simple as that. After all, you could be browsing a page on a 1600 x 1200 display on a 15-inch (38-cm) monitor or on a 640 x 480 dispay on a 21-inch (53 cm) monitor. This equates to about 40 ppi up to 120 ppi. And, of course, the end user can change their display resolution at any time, so there can be no such thing as a fixed screen resolutions to work to.

It gets worse. The 72 ppi figure is relevant because it refers to the way that Apple chose to interpret point sizes—effectively mapping one point to one pixel. The problem is that Microsoft chose a different default screen resolution of 96 ppi. What this means in practice is that Mac text uses fewer pixels for any given size and so type appears around 25% smaller!

All in all, it's a horrible mess. The physical size of your type can vary by a factor of three across display set-ups. You can guarantee that users of the two major computer platforms will be seeing radically different results.

So, is there anything that you can do? Again, we will learn later how you can gain some real control over type size, but for the moment the best thing to do is accept the inevitability of relativity. Think positively: this relativity provides a solution of sorts. If your type seems too small or too large, the end user always has the opportunity to change the default size in their browser.

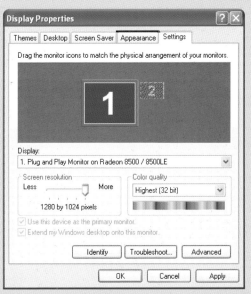

1

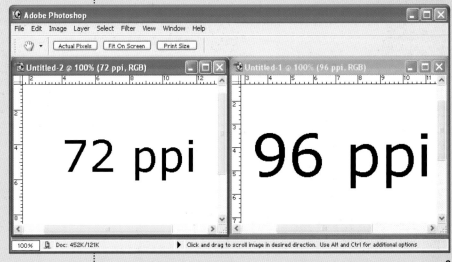

2

Netscape 4.x - Mac

This is a screen grab of what normal, default text looks like on a Mac screen

This paragraph of text has been set with various type specifications to show the differences in the overall look and readability. The text settings are, of course, dependent on the fonts being available on your system.

The size of the fonts will vary depending on your computer platform and screen resolution. The default 'normal' sizes are also reproduced from screen grabs made from Netscape and MsIE on Mac and PC systems for comparison.

MsIE 4.x - Mac

The Explorer version is almost identical but note the larger paragraph indent produced with a run of spaces and non-breaking spaces

This paragraph of text has been set with various type specifications to show the differences in the overall look and readability. The text settings are, of course, dependent on the fonts being available on your system.

The size of the fonts will vary depending on your computer platform and screen resolution. The default 'normal' sizes are also reproduced from screen grabs made from Netscape and MsIE on Mac and PC systems for comparison.

Netscape 4.x - PC

Even with the fonts size set to Small Fonts, the PC fonts are much larger. Equivalent to +1 size on a Macintosh

This paragraph of text has been set with various type specifications to show the differences in the overall look and readability. The text settings are, of course, dependent on the fonts being available on your system.

The size of the fonts will vary depending on your computer platform and screen resolution. The default 'normal' sizes are also reproduced from screen grabs made from Netscape and MsIE on Mac and PC systems for comparison.

MsIE 4.x - PC

The PC Explorer text is absolutely identical to the Netscape one

This paragraph of text has been set with various type specifications to sho and readability. The dependent on the f

The size of the computer platform 'normal' sizes are al made from Netscap for comparison.

3

1 *Display resolution—the physical size of your type onscreen—will vary across different devices. In fact, the type size can also vary if the device has a multiscan monitor supporting different resolutions.*

2 *When displaying text in the same font at the same size, Mac type (at 72 ppi) appears considerably smaller than type on a PC (at 96 ppi.)*

3 *This is particularly significant for the smaller sizes of body text. Visit www.wpdfd.com to see screenshots of the same text taken on a Mac and on a PC. The first two paragraphs show the Mac's default type size—almost unreadable.*

4 *If you, as the author, increase the type size to compensate, the problem is that it will then look too large on the PC. As the PC is the more common platform, it's better to leave your default untouched and let Mac users change their browser settings.*

4

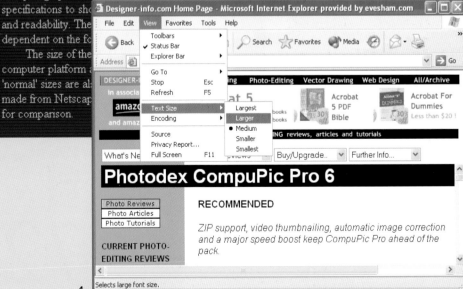

Selects large font size.

40 SCREEN TYPE QUALITY

There's another even more important factor that depends on the screen resolution: type quality.

These days, even the cheapest laser printers and inkjets can output print at 600 dpi (dots per inch), which means that there are 360,000 dots (600 x 600) per square inch to play with. Obviously, this is more than enough to produce all those subtle typographic features you might choose such as varying line widths and angled serifs.

On the Web, however, text is rendered at either 72 or 96 ppi (pixels per inch). At 72 ppi, this means just 5184 pixels (72 x 72) to do the same job, and that's about a 70th of the total of even average-quality print!

In fact, that's still enough pixels to do some justice to the subtleties of headings at a reasonable point size. But as the type gets smaller, there are fewer and fewer pixels to play with. At body text sizes, the available grid of pixels is so small that the only option is to produce the glyphs as fixed-width monolines where stems, ascenders, descenders, and so on are all a spidery 1-pixel wide. For smaller type, even this crude outline is in danger of breaking down.

This might seem the final straw. There's no point talking about the typographical niceties of different typefaces when the medium simply can't support them. More to the point, there's little scope for using other typographical tricks to enhance your message if your body text isn't even readable!

Clearly something needs to be done...

3

1

12 points

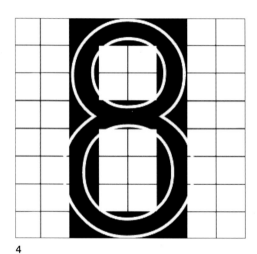

4

5

1 *Zoom in to four times actual size on some 72-point type produced at 600 ppi and the quality of the type is apparent—you can see just how many pixels go in to make the smooth serif feature on the Times New Roman typeface's "p."*

2 *Zoom in by the same factor on the same type size, this time produced at 72 dpi, and the individual pixels soon become apparent.*

3 *The situation is even worse for 12-point type at the same 72 dpi (here zoomed in to 1000%). Here, each glyph is made up of only a handful of pixels, so trying to honor the features of this Times New Roman letter shape with its angled serifs is impossible. In fact, trying to honor them just makes things worse—look how ugly the "2" has become.*

4|5 *It's a straightforward principle—the quality of the type depends on the number of pixels in the screen's bitmap grid. The more pixels there are, the more subtle the typography can be. The problem is simple too—the screen just doesn't have enough pixels.*

42 FONT SMOOTHING

The limited pixel resolution of screen output compared to print is a huge problem for type quality. In other ways, though, the screen's use of pixels offers a number of advantages over paper. In particular, unlike print where each dot of ink can only be "on" or "off," each onscreen pixel can be any of over 16 million colors.

As well as making the production of colored type much easier, this provides another huge advantage—"anti-aliasing." This works by producing intermediate shades around the edges of letters, where the typeface outline doesn't quite match the screen's pixel grid. In this way, the eye is fooled into seeing much smoother type—as if it were being produced at a much higher resolution.

This optical illusion works well to improve the quality of type above a certain size, but it has a major drawback. For smaller point sizes, where the glyphs are being produced with one-pixel strokes, any changes in the color of the stroke looks dreadful. To avoid this, most fonts have a threshold before smoothing kicks in, usually when the letter stroke rises to two pixels.

In other words, font smoothing is ideal for boosting the quality of larger type, but for body text, where the higher quality offered by anti-aliasing is needed most, the system is no longer useful. Clearly, we need another solution to ensure that our all-important copy is as readable as possible!

1

2

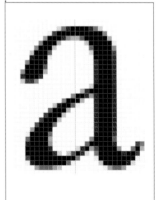

1 *Under a modern OS like Windows XP, font smoothing is built in, with two versions to choose from: standard anti-aliasing, or ClearType.*

2 | 3 *Zooming in reveals that anti-aliasing creates the illusion of smoother type using grayscales. The color fringe produced with ClearType shows that it is working at the sub-pixel level of the individual red, green, and blue phosphors. Generally, anti-aliasing is preferable, but ClearType can be useful with smaller LCD displays. These are increasingly common in the mobile age.*

4 *Zooming in to the pixel level reveals exactly how anti-aliasing works its smoothing effect.*

5 *The problem is that at small body text sizes, anti-aliasing interferes with legibility.*

3

4 No Anti-Aliasing
Anti-Aliasing

Anti-Aliasing
Anti-Aliasing

at small font sizes smoothing actually makes the type look worse

at small font sizes smoothing actually makes the type look worse

at small font sizes smoothing actually makes the type look worse

at small font sizes smoothing actually makes the type look worse

5

44 SCREEN OPTIMIZED FONTS

Font smoothing helps improve the quality of larger display type. However, for the all-important body copy, the only viable solution is to accept the constraints of the screen and to work within them.

What we need are body fonts specifically designed to look as good as possible when created at very low resolutions. In fact, we need them to look good when there are only enough pixels to enable the strokes of the font to be one pixel wide!

1

Garamond at 72

Garamond at 10

2

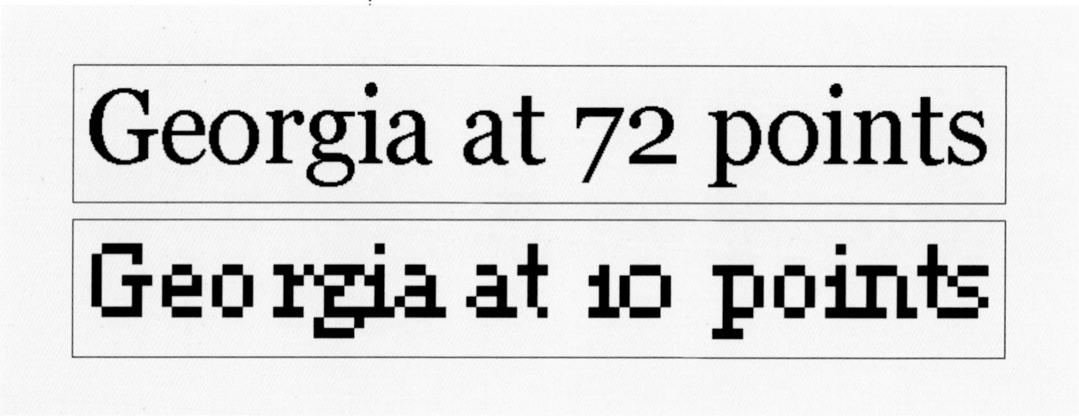

Georgia at 72 points

Georgia at 10 points

3

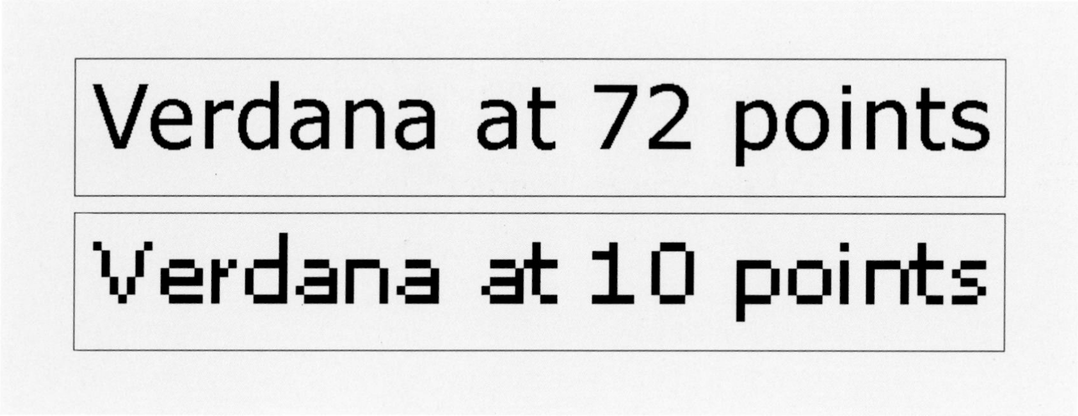

Verdana at 72 points

Verdana at 10 points

3 *It's the same with Verdana, which also dispenses with the attempt to add subtleties such as serifs, concentrating instead on producing the most legible letter shapes.*

4 *These optimized screen fonts have another trick up their sleeve—hinting. Notice how some of the letter shapes actually change at different type sizes so that you know that your type will look as good as the combination of type size and screen grid offers.*

Bearing this in mind, it would really make more sense to hand-craft the font to fit the pixel grid rather than retrospectively trying to map an outline onto it. But then, as we've just discovered, you can't actually specify an exact point size, because it's up to the platform and end user just how many pixels there are to play with.

This is where "hinting" comes in. It's a technology specially designed to take a scalable outline and to map it intelligently to the pixel grid at any given size, even radically changing the shape of type where this improves appearance. In other words, hinting provides the best of both worlds: scalability and hand-crafting.

To make the most of every pixel and to boost readability, we have to make use of those fonts specifically designed to work onscreen at small sizes. The choice isn't enormous and essentially boils down to those old serif and sans favorites Times New Roman and Arial, and the more recent Georgia and Verdana. The good news is that Microsoft has put a lot of effort into maximizing their onscreen quality—and they are freely available.

For reasonably large display type, the world is your oyster when it comes to typefaces (although there are plenty of other hurdles to overcome first). For the all-important body copy, however, we are best off sticking to these safe Web fonts - at least until screen resolution rises to meet the challenge.

Verdana at 11 points

Verdana at 12 points

Verdana at 13 points

Verdana at 14 points

1 *Beautiful typefaces such as Garamond look fine at larger sizes, but just don't translate well to the screen display's low resolution at smaller sizes.*

2 *Changing the font to Georgia makes a huge improvement in terms of legibility. The letter shapes and letter spacing have been optimized to look their best on the low-resolution pixel grid.*

4

Verdana at 11 points
Verdana at 12 points
Verdana at 13 points
Verdana at 14 points

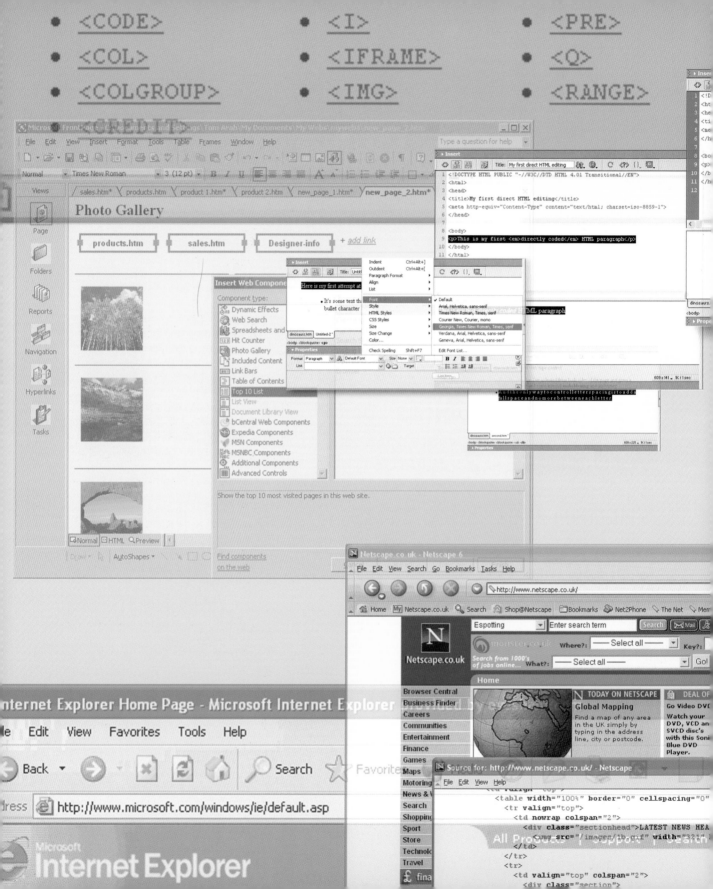

- `<VAR>`
- `<WBR>`

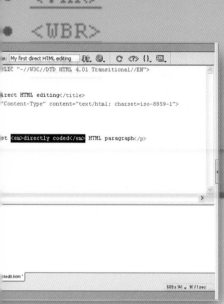

CHAPTER 3

HTML foundations

The screen is certainly not the ideal typographic medium, but once its constraints are understood, it does provide a platform on which we can build. Before we can do that, however, we have to get to grips with the other foundation of the Web, namely the code on which every webpage is built: HTML (Hypertext Markup Language).

In many ways, this is a similar story to the screen. In particular, before we can take things further and move onto the next level, we have to understand what HTML is, how it works, and what challenges it sets the budding Web typographer.

....

INTRODUCING HTML

Every single page on the Web is built on the same foundation. If you open any page in your browser and select the *View Source* or *View Page Source* command, you'll see that the page is actually built on a stream of text code. It's this code that the browser interprets to reproduce the page onscreen. And each of the billions of pages out there is built on the same code: HTML.

HTML stands for HyperText Markup Language. It and the World Wide Web itself were the inventions of the UK's Tim Berners-Lee back in 1989. It might look intimidating, but don't be put off: it's actually a lot simpler than it first appears. If you look closely at the source code, you'll see the same text content that you'd see onscreen in the browser, surrounded by other text marked off in angled brackets. This text in the angled brackets is called a "tag." Each tag is repeated before and after the content, the closing tag having a forward slash before the tag name. For example, <tagname> visible text content </tagname>. It's by interpreting these tags that the browser determines how to present the content contained within, and it's the use of these tags that makes HTML a mark-up language.

HTML is a beautifully simple system, and simplicity is the secret of the Web's success. Using HTML, anyone can produce a webpage (and millions already have!) All that you have to remember is not to be afraid of the code.

Contents	See also

Tim Berners-Lee

Weaving the Web by Tim Berners-Lee with Mark Fischetti, (Harper San Francisco; Hardback: ISBN:0062515861, Abridged audio cassette abridged ISBN:0694521256) and various other languages.

Bio

A graduate of Oxford University, England, Tim now holds the 3Com Founders chair at the Laboratory for Computer Science (LCS)at the Massachusetts Institute of Technology (MIT). He directs the World Wide Web Consortium, an open forum of companies and organizations with the mission to lead the Web to its full potential.

With a background of system design in real-time communications and text processing software development, in 1989 he invented the World Wide Web, an internet-based hypermedia initiative for global information sharing. while working at CERN, the European Particle Physics Laboratory. He wrote the first web client (browser-editor) and server in 1990.

Before coming to CERN, Tim worked with Image Computer Systems, of Ferndown, Dorset, England and before that a principal engineer with

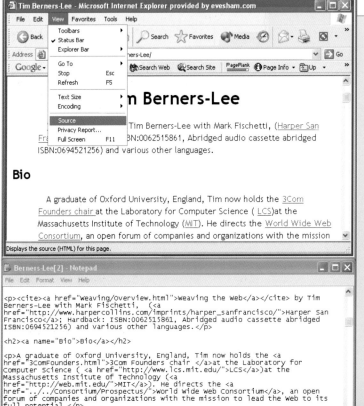

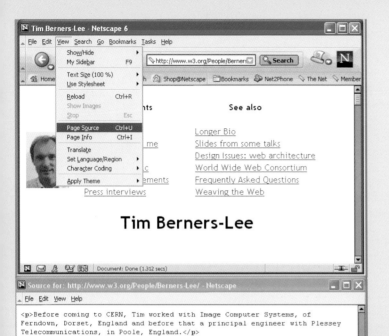

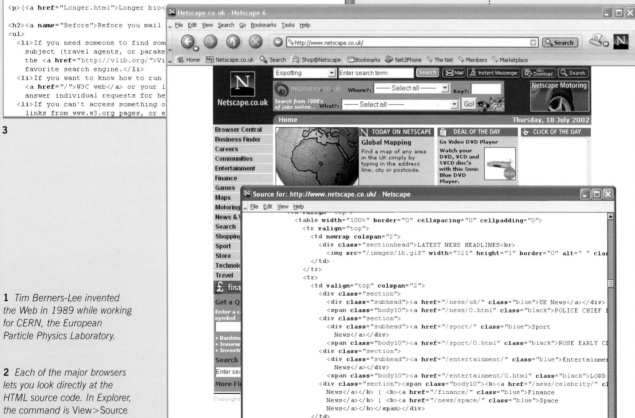

3 *In Navigator the command is* View> Page Source, *and the code is loaded into a dedicated viewing window. This is particularly useful as the HTML syntax is color-coded—the page content is in ordinary black and the HTML tags are in purple.*

4 *For more advanced pages, the code becomes more complex, but the same approach of HTML tags surrounding content applies.*

1 *Tim Berners-Lee invented the Web in 1989 while working for CERN, the European Particle Physics Laboratory.*

2 *Each of the major browsers lets you look directly at the HTML source code. In Explorer, the command is* View>Source *and the code is automatically loaded into Notepad.*

50 HTML TAGGING

HTML is the mark-up language, but what exactly does it mark up? From the typographer's point-of-view, it would be great if HTML marked up type formatting so that we could quickly tag a heading to make it 32 point Futura bold with 36-point leading and a three-point ruling line above.

Sadly, HTML wasn't created with the designer in mind. Instead, HTML was created as a medium for scientists exchanging information in technical documents. And to the scientist, any fancy formatting could actually interfere with the transmission of information. The end result was that HTML was deliberately intended as a design-free zone. What mattered to Berners-Lee was content, and style didn't come second—it came nowhere!

Rather than being concerned with presentation, the HTML tags are all about content. Rather than formatting tags, HTML consists of a set of so-called "logical" tags. If you want to mark off a quotation, for example, you simply put an opening <blockquote> tag before the text and a closing </blockquote> tag after. Likewise, if you want to emphasize some text in a paragraph, you put a <strong> tag before it and a closing </strong> tag after.

The good news is that Tim Berners-Lee knew that HTML had to be simple and efficient to be popular, so the number of core HTML tags is limited.

1 *Taking a close-up view of the HTML source code gives us more of an idea of how it works. The tags aren't precise formatting instructions, but rather, logical mark-ups. In this section of code, there's an <h1> and <h2>heading tag, a couple of <p> default paragraph tags, four <a> hyperlinks (the <a> actually stands for "anchor"), and a <cite> tag for marking off citations that reference books or other works.*

2 *When interpreted by the browser, this is how Internet Explorer presents the code. As you can see, the simple mark-up instructions have turned our text into something a little more navigable!*

Tim Berners-Lee

Weaving the Web by Tim Berners-Lee with Mark Fischetti, (Harper San Francisco; Hardback: ISBN:0062515861, Abridged audio cassette abridged ISBN:0694521256) and various other languages.

2

```
<h1>Tim Berners-Lee</h1>

<p><a href="2001/MLD"></a></p>

<p><cite><a href="Weaving/Overview.html">Weaving th
Berners-Lee with Mark Fischetti,  (<a
href="http://www.harpercollins.com/imprints/harper_
Francisco</a>; Hardback: ISBN:0062515861, Abridged
ISBN:0694521256) and various other languages.</p>
```

1

3

Compact Index of HTML Tags

This compact index of tags is arranged alphabetically. Each tag is a link that leads to a description of the tag and its syntax. If you need more detail, try the complete index that also includes tag names. Four other indexes are available that list tags according to the standards they support.

Willcam's Comprehensive HTML Cross Reference was created as a service to the Internet community, and forms part of Willcam's Internet and HTML curriculum. It represents a joint effort of The Willcam Group and Gregory Consulting and is Copyright 1995 and 1996, The Willcam Group Limited. Please report any errors or omissions to Kate Gregory.

- <!-->
- <
- <A>
- <ABBREV>
- <ACRONYM>
- <ADDRESS>
- <APPLET>
- <AREA>
- <AU>
- <AUTHOR>
- <B>
- <BANNER>
- <BASE>
- <BASEFONT>
- <BGSOUND>
- <BIG>
- <BLINK>
- <BLOCKQUOTE>
- <BQ>
- <BODY>
-
- <CAPTION>
- <CENTER>
- <CITE>
- <CODE>
- <COL>
- <COLGROUP>
- <CREDIT>

- <DEL>
- <DFN>
- <DIR>
- <DIV>
- <DL>
- <DT>
- <DD>
- <EM>
- <EMBED>
- <FIG>
- <FN>
- <FONT>
- <FORM>
- <FRAME>
- <FRAMESET>
- <H1>
- <H2>
- <H3>
- <H4>
- <H5>
- <H6>
- <HEAD>
- <HR>
- <HTML>
- <I>
- <IFRAME>
- <IMG>

- <INPUT>
- <INS>
- <ISINDEX>
- <KBD>
- <LANG>
- <LH>
- <LI>
- <LINK>
- <LISTING>
- <MAP>
- <MARQUEE>
- <MATH>
- <MENU>
- <META>
- <MULTICOL>
- <NOBR>
- <NOFRAMES>
- <NOTE>
- <OL>
- <OVERLAY>
- <P>
- <PARAM>
- <PERSON>
- <PLAINTEXT>
- <PRE>
- <Q>
- <RANGE>

- <SAMP>
- <SCRIPT>
- <SELECT>
- <SMALL>
- <SPACER>
- <SPOT>
- <STRIKE>
- <STRONG>
- <SUB>
- <SUP>
- <TAB>
- <TABLE>
- <TBODY>
- <TD>
- <TEXTAREA>
- <TEXTFLOW>
- <TFOOT>
- <TH>
- <THEAD>
- <TITLE>
- <TR>
- <TT>
- <U>
- <UL>
- <VAR>
- <WBR>
- <XMP>

</a></cite> by Tim

ancisco/">Harper San
   cassette abridged

3 There are just over 100 HTML tags in existence and you can find them listed on numerous websites. The majority are rarely used and many are "deprecated," which means that you should avoid using them. The core range of tags we'll be handling is actually far smaller—about 25.

4 Different webpage authoring applications provide different levels of tagging help. Dreamweaver MX is the most helpful with its dedicated Tag Chooser facility.

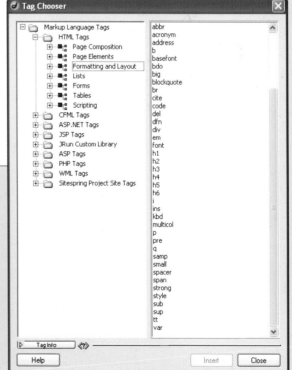

4

52

INTRODUCING
THE BROWSER

Every webpage may be built on HTML code, but the Web wouldn't be the medium it is today if every page was just a stream of unformatted text. Instead, each page's HTML code is interpreted and formatted by a special piece of software—the Web browser—before being displayed to the end user.

The first mass-market Web browser back in the early 1990s was called Mosaic, and this later developed into Netscape Navigator. Microsoft belatedly recognized the threat this posed and came up with its own browser, Internet Explorer. Netscape and Explorer have since fought it out for dominance, with Explorer the clear winner; but both browsers still claim significant market share alongside smaller players, such as the popular Opera.

Whichever browser your site's visitors use, it plays a crucial role because the browser itself chooses how to interpret each of those HTML logical tags. Thankfully, there's a lot of shared ground, so that both Netscape and Explorer indent the <blockquote> tag, for example, and embolden the <strong> tag.

Even so, there's still a huge amount of room for difference, not just between the major browsers, but between the same browser on the Mac and PC platforms (and even between different versions of the same browser on the same platform!). The result is a recipe for confusion, and every day a thousand Web designers are reduced to tears by these annoying browser differences.

There *are* ways to minimize the impact of browser differences, but this is another case where the best policy is to accept some relativity as inevitable.

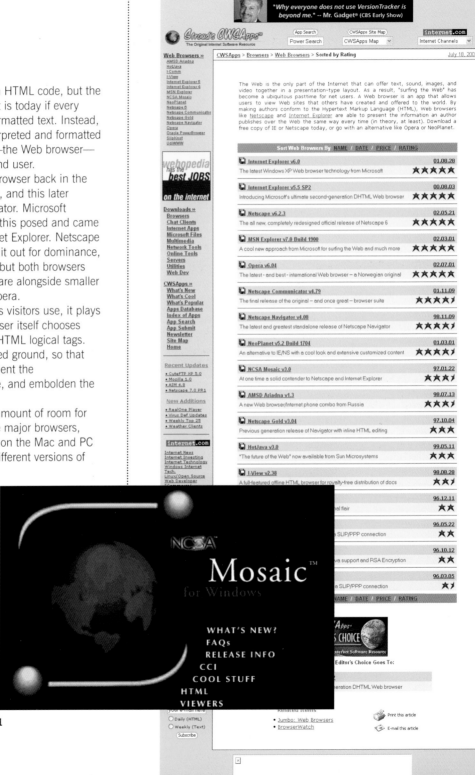

1

2

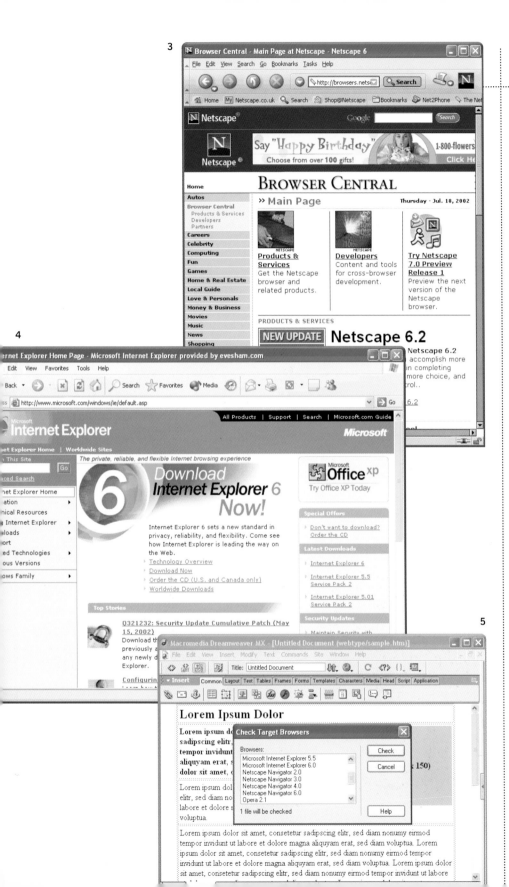

1 *NCSA Mosaic was the first widely and freely available browser and it kickstarted the Web revolution.*

2 *Mosaic and a whole host of other browsers, such as Opera and NeoPlanet, are available directly on the Web from sites like* http://cws.internet.com.

3 *These days, there are two main contenders: Netscape Navigator, available from* www.netscape.com...

4 *...and Microsoft Internet Explorer, available from* www.microsoft.com. *Of the two, Internet Explorer is now generally recognized as the more powerful and is certainly the more popular.*

5 *Matters are complicated by the fact that each release of each browser has different capabilities. The best solution is to make sure you test your site with the latest version of both major browsers. And, if your Web authoring application provides the capability, check your pages against previous release specifications.*

54 WEB AUTHORING APPS

Browsers take care of displaying webpages, so how do you go about creating them? Fortunately, the simplicity of HTML's tagging system and its text-based nature mean that anyone with access to a computer can produce a webpage. All that you need is a text editor, such as Word or Notepad, that can save text with no formatting information (this is usually referred to as ascii format).

This will provide you with the minimum that you need, but thankfully there are plenty of other dedicated HTML authoring packages to choose between. Of these, there are three packages that dominate the market.

The first is Microsoft's FrontPage, which is aimed at the occasional Web user. FrontPage tends to play down direct HTML editing in favor of a more visual DTP-style approach, and it aims to get users off to a flying start.

The second is Adobe's GoLive, which is aimed at the print-oriented designer. GoLive attempts to take the same professional design-rich expertise that Adobe has built up with its other applications—InDesign, Illustrator, PageMaker, and Photoshop—and transfer it to the Web.

The third application is Macromedia Dreamweaver. This was the first program to encourage both visual, page-based layout and code-based editing, and it still leads the pack on both fronts. Dreamweaver and its associated applications, Fireworks and Flash (available together in the Studio MX suite), make the perfect platform for professional Web authoring.

If you are serious about becoming a Web type expert, Dreamweaver stands out as the best current choice (check for educational pricing and second-hand deals on eBay if the price is offputting!). Remember, though, that every webpage is built on the same HTML foundations. Theoretically, you could produce exactly the same code in GoLive, FrontPage, or even WordPad as you can in Dreamweaver.

Whichever package you choose you can take control of your type.

1

2

3

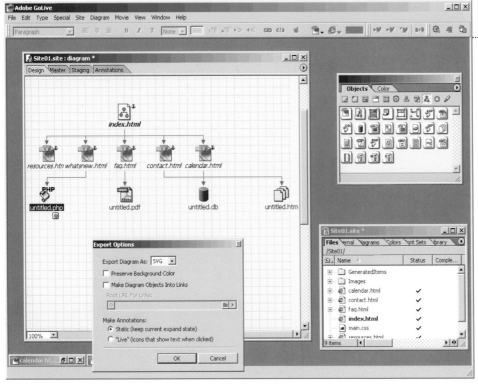

1 *You can produce a webpage using just a basic text editor.*

2 *FrontPage is aimed at occasional users who want to produce impressive results quickly—but it's not for the expert or aspirational user.*

3 *GoLive is a professional package aimed primarily at print-oriented designers, especially existing Adobe users who want to move their work onto the Web.*

4 *Dreamweaver MX currently dominates the world of webpage creation, much as Photoshop does for image-creation and editing.*

5 *Here the Amazon.com home page is being edited in FrontPage 2002 to show that, thanks to the underlying HTML architecture, any page layout can be produced in any package. You'd really be better off with a more advanced package—but it can be done!*

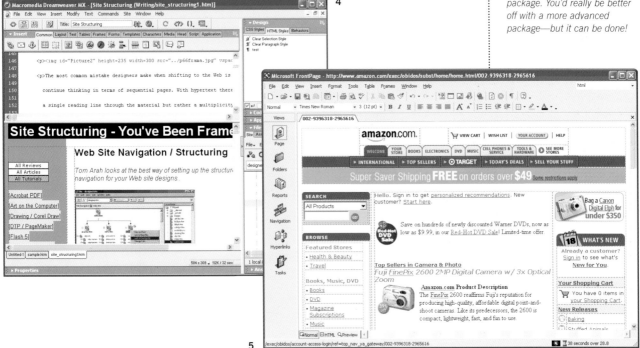

4

5

56 PROJECT 1:
QUICK START

OK. So let's load up the main Web authoring
applications and see what sort of type control they
offer out of the box. First impressions are certainly
positive, as each application offers what looks like a
pretty comprehensive type formatting system.

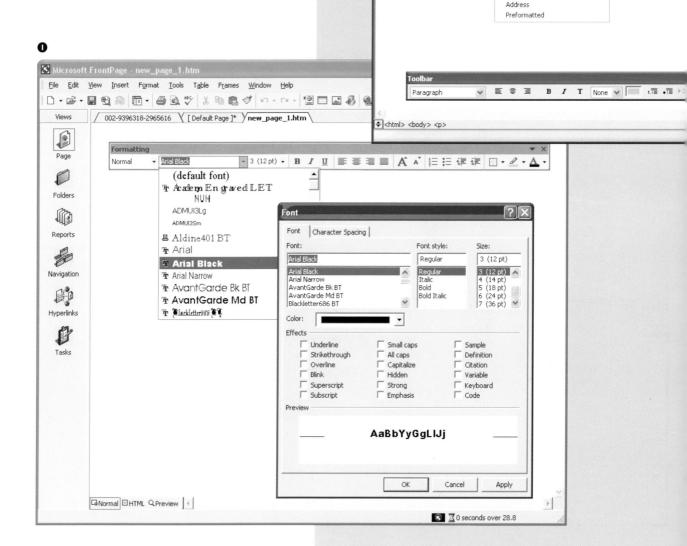

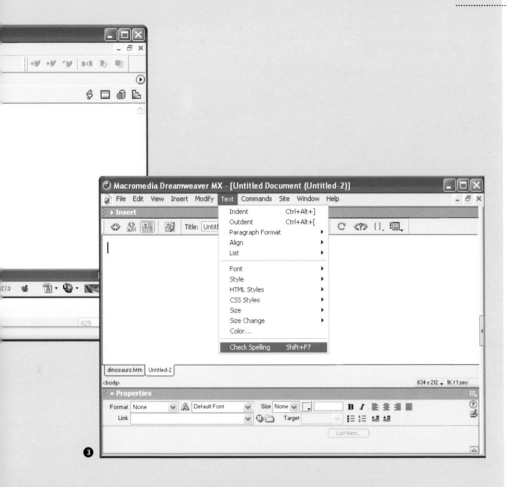

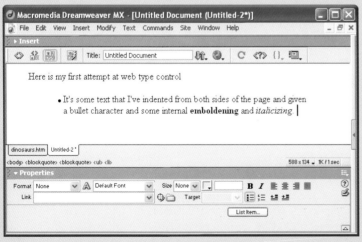

❶ FrontPage offers a formatting toolbar very similar to the one in Microsoft Word, with direct access to styles, font formatting, font sizes, emboldening, italicizing, bulleting, alignment, and the ability to increase and decrease paragraph indenting. The *Format* menu also gives access to familiar type-formatting commands, such as the *Font* dialog.

❷ GoLive offers the same common type-formatting commands directly from its main toolbar. It also offers a dedicated *Type* menu with type-formatting commands for controlling font, size, style, and so on.

❸ Dreamweaver enables its immediate type control via the context-sensitive *Properties* panel at the bottom of the screen rather than from a toolbar under the main menu. The basic type commands, though, are familiar, including all the usual suspects—paragraph styles, font formatting, font size, emboldening, italicizing, bulleting, and text indent and outdent. And like GoLive, Dreamweaver offers a dedicated *Type* menu for further control.

Using just these familiar commands, it's easy to achieve some quick results. Maybe HTML isn't such an unforgiving design medium after all…

❹ Using Dreamweaver's *Properties* panel, we can easily put some formatting together. To begin, we can indent a paragraph a couple of times, then add a bullet and turn it into bold italics. Not bad for starters.

58

The range of options might not reach the same level as DTP applications, but the similarities to wordprocessing are clear. However, let's explore further and see just how far we can go.

➎ Let's try and change the typeface. In wordprocessors, we're used to picking any typeface installed on our system. In our Web-authoring apps (with the exception of FrontPage), though it's very different. We'll come back to this throughout the book.

➏ Or how about the type size? Again from wordprocessors and DTP applications we're used to setting the point size directly but none of the authoring programs let us do this. We'll come back to this too!

➐ Or how about changing the spacing—for example, to control the spacing between letters and lines? Again, there are no obvious commands available to do this, but surely we can force some control by manually adding spaces? Well yes, but only up to a point: if you try and enter more than one space, your editor will simply ignore it!

It's clear, then, that type formatting for the Web isn't quite as simple as we thought. So let's move away from each application's WYSIWYG layout mode and take a look at the HTML code itself.

➑ One way to do this is to first load the page into your browser for previewing. This is good practice in any case as the Design view isn't a completely accurate representation of how the browser will actually interpret the page. It also means that we can view the source code just as we did earlier (see page 52).

➎

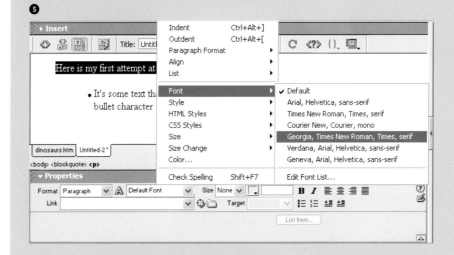

➏

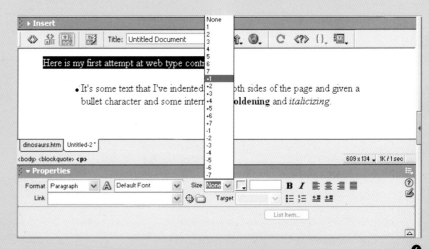

➐

8

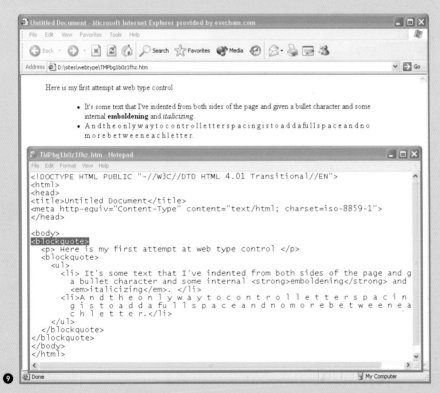

9

When we take a look at the HTML code, everything becomes a bit clearer. Although each of the Web-authoring packages seemed to promise word-processor style formatting (as we already really knew), the only way that they are able to offer any type control at all is through the use of HTML's logical tags.

9 Looking at the example we created earlier, we can see that the indenting was achieved through nesting <blockquote> tags, the bold text through <strong> tags, the italicizing through <em> tags (short for "emphasis"), and the bullets through the use of <li> list item tags nested within a <ul> unordered list tag.

There's no doubt that the wordprocessor-style shortcuts for producing HTML-based effects are extremely handy and we'll be using them a lot. But it's important to realize that, despite appearances, they don't provide the same sort of tight control as they do in a word processor or DTP application. Understanding this is important. Otherwise, the shortcuts can lead to confusion. This is particularly the case here because all the applications use shortcuts that are no longer recommended practice, and in some cases use shortcuts that are misleading and sometimes dangerous. Microsoft FrontPage, in particular, is notorious for letting you quickly apply formatting that works only in its own Microsoft Explorer browser, or only on your own system. Sadly, its own font control is a good case in point.

While word processor style formatting is convenient, there are no shortcuts to becoming a Web type expert.

60

PROJECT 2:
WORKING WITH HTML

Ultimately, to become a real Web type expert, you have to get to grips with the underlying code. Rather than pretending that Web design isn't built on HTML, let's embrace the fact and see where it takes us. It's not that difficult, especially because all the major authoring packages let you edit the code directly.

❶ We'll use Dreamweaver for most of the projects in this book. The first two buttons on the main toolbar switch between the *Design* view (where you lay out pages) and *Code* view (where you work with the HTML code itself). The third offers a split view—select text in either pane and the relevant content is displayed in the other.

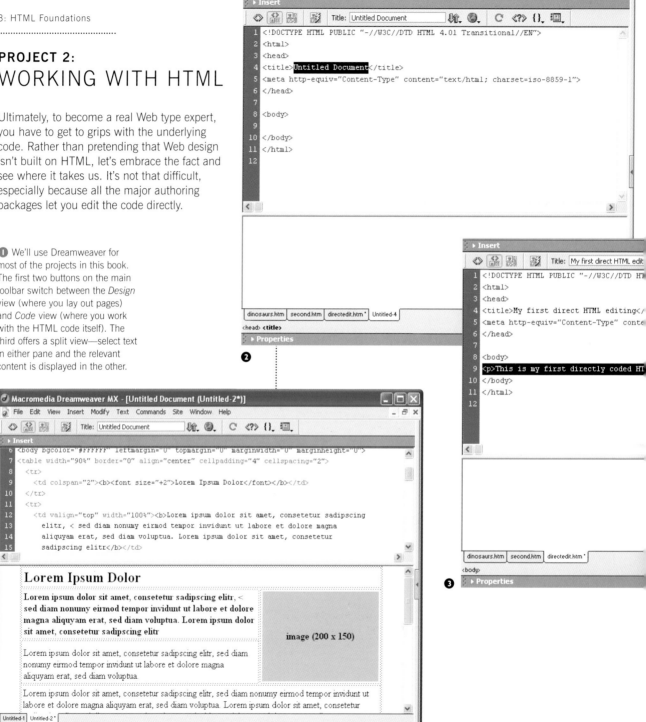

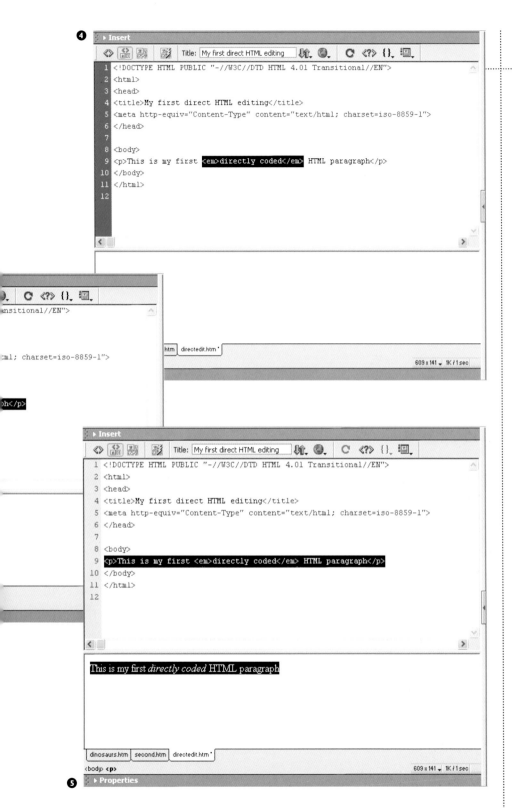

❷ The first thing to do is create a new blank page. Although the layout in the *Design* view is blank, the *HTML* window already contains some tags between the opening <head> and closing </head> tags because Just ignore the frightening looking <!DOCTYPE...> and <meta > tags for now. These are added to all pages so that the browser knows how to interpret them. Instead, we'll give our page a title by changing the text between the opening <title> and closing </title> tags. This is good practice, as it's the text that appears in the title bar of the browser, and it's also treated as the most important text on the page by search engines.

❸ The only tags that will appear onscreen in the body of our page must be added between the opening <body> and closing </body> tags, so make sure that your cursor is repositioned correctly. The basic paragraph tag is marked up with a <p> tag: remember to insert these around each new paragraph. Dreamweaver makes things easier by automatically prompting as you type and adding the closing </p>.

❹ Each <p> tag is called a "block tag" because the browser automatically forces a line break after it. HTML also supports "inline tags" within block elements. A good example is the <em> tag for adding emphasis. Select a section of your text and add an <em> tag before and a closing </em> tag afterward.

❺ Now we're ready to see some results. Click on the application's *Layout* view and it updates to reflect the changes. If mistakes have been made, don't panic: Dreamweaver will highlight them for correction.

62 PROJECT 3:
CORE HTML SHOWCASE

Now that you understand the basics of quick
HTML tagging and editing, let's put everything
together on a real project. We'll create a webpage
to advertise a music festival.

You'll notice straightaway that the webpage
we're putting together is far from the jazzy,
interactive websites you're probably familiar with
from your own Web surfing experiences. But don't
forget, we're dealing with the basics of type and
typography online at this stage, and you'll never be
able to create all the ideas you can see in your
imagination until you've covered the basics of how
type works—and doesn't work—in the Internet
environment. Be patient!

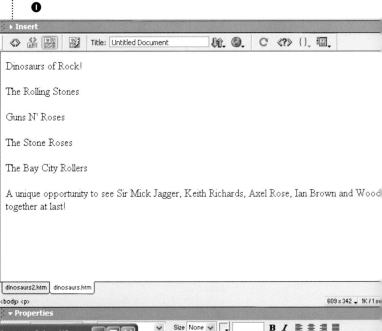

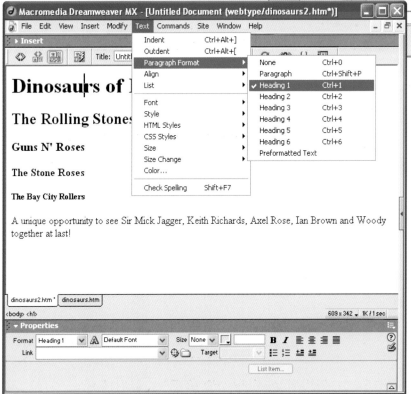

Creating a hierarchy

The first thing this enables us to explore
is the typographic feature that HTML has
always majored on: the ability to set up a
hierarchy of importance. Remember that
HTML was invented to handle scientific
information, where it's crucial to be able
to mark out headings, subheadings, sub-
subheadings, and so on. HTML provides
a range of six heading tags, <H1>
through to <H6>, for exactly this
purpose, and we can put them to use for
our festival page to mark out headline
and support acts.

We can also mark out internal points
of interest within paragraphs using inline
tags. As well as indicating relative
importance, our marked text acts to
provide possible text entry, to break up
the text, and to provide variety.

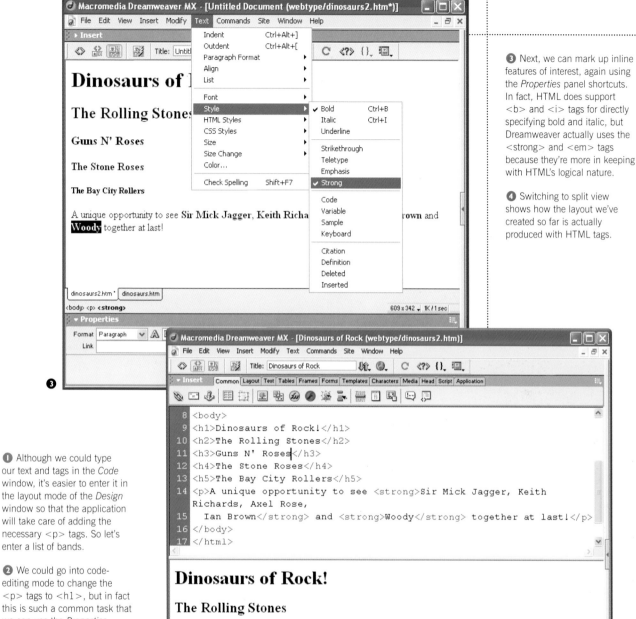

❸ Next, we can mark up inline features of interest, again using the *Properties* panel shortcuts. In fact, HTML does support `<b>` and `<i>` tags for directly specifying bold and italic, but Dreamweaver actually uses the `<strong>` and `<em>` tags because they're more in keeping with HTML's logical nature.

❹ Switching to split view shows how the layout we've created so far is actually produced with HTML tags.

❶ Although we could type our text and tags in the *Code* window, it's easier to enter it in the layout mode of the *Design* window so that the application will take care of adding the necessary `<p>` tags. So let's enter a list of bands.

❷ We could go into code-editing mode to change the `<p>` tags to `<h1>`, but in fact this is such a common task that we can use the *Properties* panel, or choose commands from the *Type* menu, or use the context-sensitive right-click menu. Again, these have the advantage that the application automatically changes both opening and closing tags for you. As you would expect, the resulting headings are all bold and ordered in terms of size.

64 Creating interest

So far so good, but we need to add some color. You might not think of the space surrounding your type in terms of color, but controlling this "white space" in your layout is a crucial typographic tool. Our options here are very limited, but, we can at least indent paragraphs from either side as we saw earlier. We can also create graphical interest with some bullets and rules. Finally, we can pull out all the stops by changing the color of our page and text.

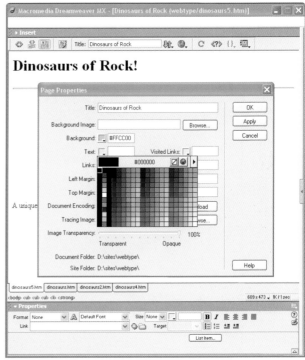

❺ Using the *Properties* panel's *Text Indent* command, we can quickly add multiple nested <blockquote> tags to open up some surrounding space and add variety.

❻ Add <hr> horizontal rules and break up the main paragraph into a bulleted unordered <ol> list. To do this, use the commands under the *Insert* and *Text> List* menus. All this will add some basic graphical interest.

❼ Using the *Modify>Page Properties* command, we can choose an overall background color and a color for our text.

❽ Switching to *Code* view, we can see the HTML tags that define our layout.

❾ And by previewing the page in a browser, we can see how it appears to the end user.

8

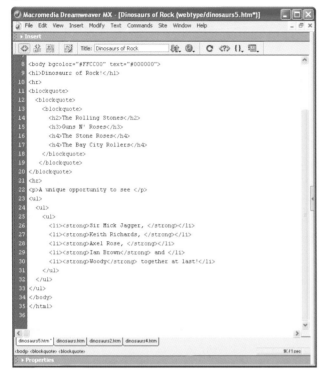

9

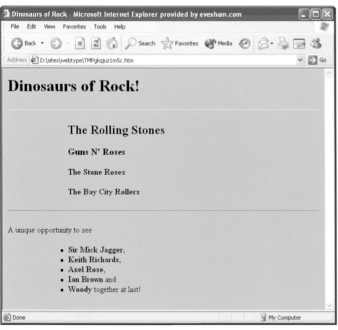

Where we stand

The end result has some interest and some chance of attracting the visitor and keeping them reading. It shows HTML doing exactly what it was intended to do: marking out a relative hierarchy of information. We should also remind ourselves that it is precisely because HTML was conceived in this simple, almost design-free way that the Web exists for us to complain about!

That's the positive spin. Now let's face the facts. We have no way of precisely setting or changing our type's face, size, style, spacing, alignment, or layout. All those centuries building up typefaces and the typographic know-how needed to make the most of them—and all those recent expectations raised by print-oriented DTP—count for nothing. On the Web, we're suddenly restricted to a few sizes and styles of Times. And we're not even really in control of these, as the final appearance of the page and its type is actually determined by the user and their browser.

At this stage, you'd be forgiven for wondering whether it would be possible to invent a less promising medium for type control. Don't give up hope: there's plenty more that we can do to seize back control. Even better, having these basics under our belt is an essential first step to moving on. Understanding, appreciating, and taking control of the core HTML tags and principles underpins all Web typography, including the most modern formatting solutions.

You might not think it now, but eventually you'll bless Tim Berners-Lee for his decision to keep HTML concentrated on handling content and to leave formatting to one side.

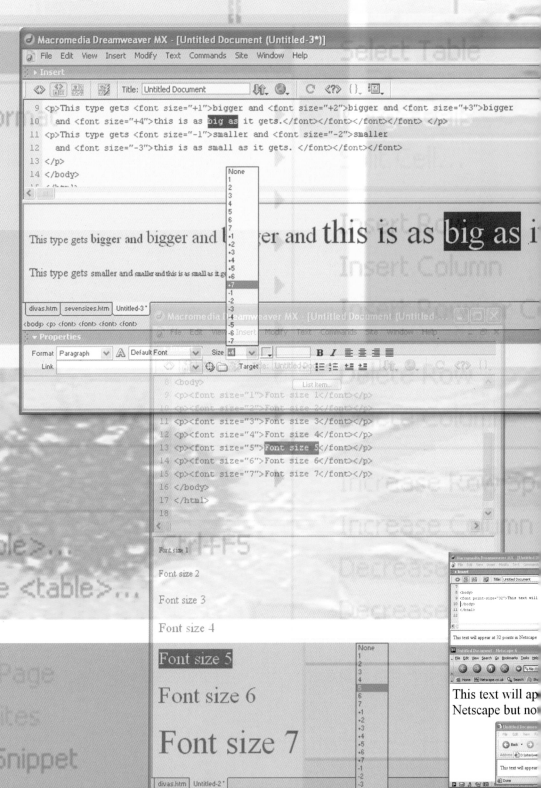

C H A P T E R 4

Extending HTML

HTML made the Web possible, but its focus on scientific content meant that its design capabilities were limited. Designers are nothing if not ingenious, however, and they soon adapted existing HTML features to new ends. Meanwhile Netscape and Microsoft were looking for ways to make their browsers stand out. Adding design-focused proprietary tags was an excellent way to gain an edge.

Eventually the best of these became so established that they were built into a new specification which all today's browsers fully support. HTML 3.2 is the design secret behind the majority of current web sites and the one which we'll explore in this chapter.

68 PROJECT 4:
TYPE LAYOUT CONTROL

The most immediate need of any designer is to gain some kind of layout control. After all, the typographic feature that most determines readability (after the legibility of the typeface) is line length. However, the reflowing nature of basic HTML makes these design considerations entirely dependent on the size of the screen and the browser window.

Designers have work this around by using HTML's <table> tag—which was originally intended for producing scientific tables—to create a grid for the page as a whole.

Let's see how this can be used to add a multi-column layout to our existing music festival page—and to control the body copy's width.

The page grid <table> workaround described here is by no means ideal: the code can get complex and therefore difficult to edit and slow for the browser to interpret. It also doesn't support features such as flowing, newspaper-style columns. For the moment, though, let's appreciate the fact that we've finally got some layout control!

In fact, the table framework proves to be surprisingly powerful. Using exactly the same skills that you learn here—controlling the numbers of rows and columns, setting percentage and pixel widths, and merging cells—you can create any of the advanced layouts that you see on the Web. It's easy.

❶

❶ To add the table, hit the *Insert>Table* command and specify a two-row by three-column table with cell padding set to eight pixels. Change the width setting from *Percentage* to *Pixels* so that we can specify an exact size of 580 pixels. We're using this figure because it will fit comfortably on 640 x 480 browsers without the need for a horizontal scrollbar.

❷ Now turn the table into a layout grid by merging the two cells on the right of the top row and then pasting in the existing text. Having done so, add some brand new text into the two cells of the first column.

❷

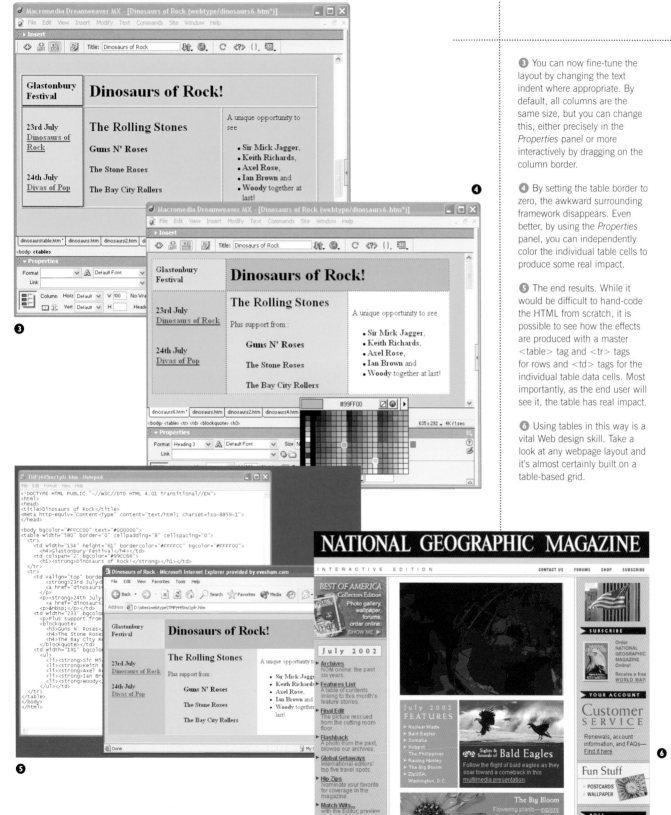

3 You can now fine-tune the layout by changing the text indent where appropriate. By default, all columns are the same size, but you can change this, either precisely in the *Properties* panel or more interactively by dragging on the column border.

4 By setting the table border to zero, the awkward surrounding framework disappears. Even better, by using the *Properties* panel, you can independently color the individual table cells to produce some real impact.

5 The end results. While it would be difficult to hand-code the HTML from scratch, it is possible to see how the effects are produced with a master <table> tag and <tr> tags for rows and <td> tags for the individual table data cells. Most importantly, as the end user will see it, the table has real impact.

6 Using tables in this way is a vital Web design skill. Take a look at any webpage layout and it's almost certainly built on a table-based grid.

70 PROJECT 5:
TYPE SIZE CONTROL

The <table> tag provides Web layout control. But what about type? For typographic control, the solution that designers and browser developers came up with is the catch-all <font> tag and its various attributes.

The first typographic feature we want to control is the type size, and the <font> tag seems to offer the perfect attribute with its "point-size" option. Sadly this is a Netscape-only attribute and we can't afford to ignore the majority (who are Explorer users).

Fortunately there's another <font> attribute that is universally supported: "size." The problem is that unlike point-size, it's not an absolute measure. An even bigger limitation is that there are only seven sizes to choose from—and it's down to the browser to decide what point-size each HTML fixed size represents. And—surprise, surprise—different browsers and even different browser versions interpret the settings differently.

The <font size> attribute isn't a final type size solution—we'll see more modern and more powerful alternatives later—but beggars can't be choosers. We'll take whatever control we're offered!

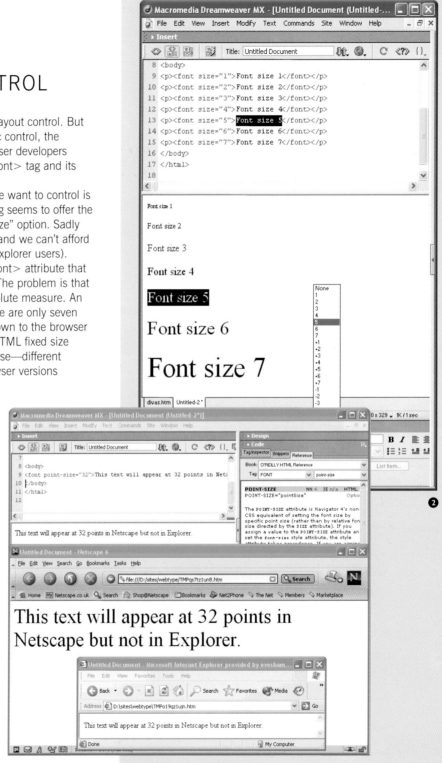

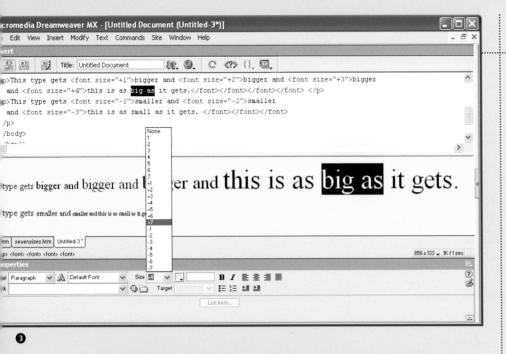

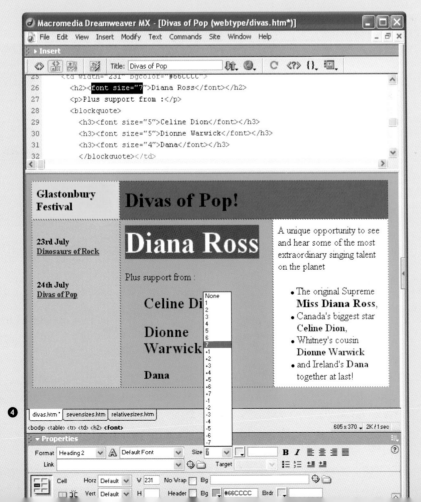

① The <font> tag's point-size attribute works in Netscape but is ignored within Explorer.

② To explore the seven possible sizes of the <font> tag, create seven paragraphs and then apply each fixed size from the *Properties* palette.

③ Font sizes can also be applied inline within a paragraph and sizes can be made relative: e.g. "+1," "-3", and so on. As the usual default size is three, that leaves two smaller variations and four larger ones. Remember that the end user can also also raise or lower the default type size.

④ To put <font> sizes to use on a real project, you can duplicate the grid layout we created earlier and edit it to produce some new copy. This time, we can override the in-built heading sizes to ensure the desired fixed font size. Another advantage is that the largest font size, seven, is actually bigger than the default <h1> setting. We can also use relative font sizes to shrink the size of the links to stop them distracting from the main copy.

72 PROJECT 6:

TYPEFACE CONTROL

As well as relative type size control, the <font> tag also lets us take some control over typeface with its "face" attribute. In fact, using the direct HTML editing that we saw earlier, you can simply specify any font on your system—<font face="anyface"> text </font>—and it will appear on your page. It's almost too easy.

And, unfortunately, it is. The font isn't actually included in the page because we're working in simple, text-only HTML code. The font appears as specified because it's installed and ready to go on your system, but you can't assume that the same will be true for every one of your site's end users. And, if it isn't, your carefully chosen typeface will default back to the browser's default and you're back to square one.

So what's the way forward? The first is to make sure that you stick to the fonts that your site visitors are most likely to have. The second is to realize that you can specify more than one font at a time. If the first font isn't available, the browser tries the second, then the third, and so on. And just in case the end user's system doesn't have any of your choices installed, you can set a generic last option of "serif" or "sans-serif" that the browser will honor.

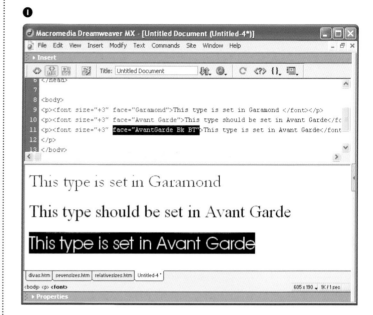

❶

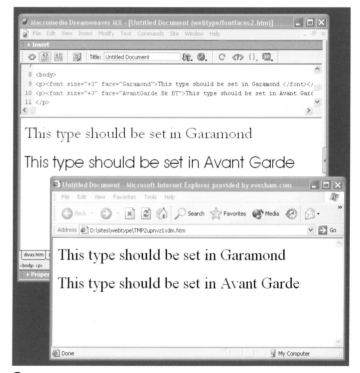

❷

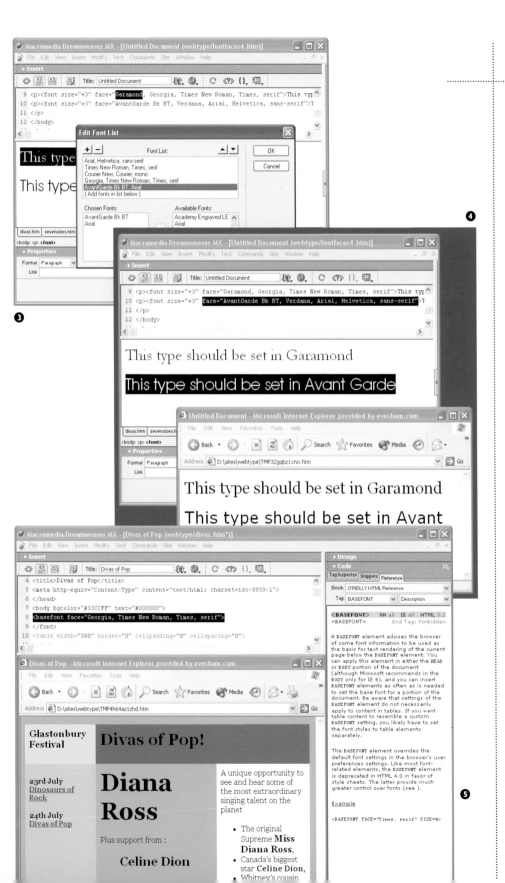

❶ By directly editing the <font> tag, you can specify any font and, if it is installed on your system, it will appear. Make sure that you specify the font name exactly as it appears in the *Font* selection dialog.

❷ Crucially though, you can't expect your end user to see the same fonts that you do—you can't control which fonts they have installed. If they don't have your chosen font, the face reverts to the browser default.

❸ You can specify the most common font lists directly, or you can quickly create your own with Dreamweaver's dedicated *Font List* editor or by directly editing the HTML code.

❹ Specifying font lists means that if the first font isn't installed, as here, the browser tries the second, the third, and so on. There's no harm in specifying fonts that aren't installed, and this way you can set up your font choices to degrade gracefully.

❺ Specifying a <font> tag for every element would be a serious chore. A useful shortcut is to use the <basefont> tag to apply the type formatting to all text until the next <basefont> tag appears. Using this, we can change the face for our festival pages with just one line, swapping from Times New Roman to the more friendly Georgia. Be careful though: not all of the browsers handle the <basefont> tag as you'd expect, or wish. Who would have guessed?

⁷⁴ SPECIFYING COLORS

One of the big advantages of publishing to the pixel-based screen is that it's a lot easier to specify colors than it is in print. We've already seen how you can set up overall page properties, but we really want finer control than that. Again, the solution is a <font> tag attribute, in this case "color." Using <font color="…">, you can quickly change the color of any amount of text before the closing </font> tag.

So how do you specify the color you want? All color on computers is handled as mixtures of red, green, and blue (RGB). Each color component can be at one of 256 levels. When combined (256 x 256 x 256), this makes a total of 16.7 million colors to choose from. The computer handles these in hexadecimal code—the code for olive green is "808000". Obvious, really.

Fortunately, you're not expected to memorize over 16 million hexadecimal codes. Web-authoring packages let you choose colors directly, and then generate the codes for you. This has the advantage that the program can steer you to the so-called "Web-safe" colors that are natively supported by older or handheld displays limited to just 256 colors.

However, just because you can specify any color doesn't mean that you should. To begin with, you need to bear readability in mind. To make it as easy on the eye as possible, you need strong contrast—it's not an accident that the vast majority of print is black type on a white background. Also, the "less is more" principle applies to different text colors just as it does to different typefaces. Use only a couple of type colors per page—and choose them wisely if you choose them at all.

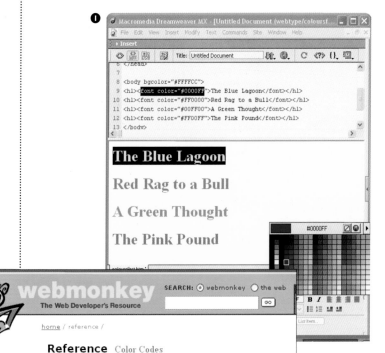

❶

Reference Color Codes

When you're adding a color to your Web page with HTML, sometimes you can just type in the name of the color. But more often than not, you'll need to use what's called the hex code, which is something that the browser will be able to understand. Choose a color from the list below and look to its left to get the hex code. If we wanted our background to be red, for example, we'd type bgcolor="#FF0000". Try it out!

If you'd like to print this chart and you are using Internet Explorer, click on "Tools" and then "Advanced." Next, scroll down to "Printing" and make sure the "Print background colors and images" box is checked.

Quick Reference:

JavaScript Library
HTML Cheatsheet
Special Characters
Color Codes
Browser Chart
Stylesheet Guide
Unix Guide
Glossary
Domain Registries

Hex Code	Color	Hex Code	Color	Hex Code	Color
#FFFFFF		#CCFFFF		#99FFFF	
#FFFFCC		#CCFFCC		#99FFCC	
#FFFF99		#CCFF99		#99FF99	
#FFFF66		#CCFF66		#99FF66	
#FFFF33		#CCFF33		#99FF33	
#FFFF00		#CCFF00		#99FF00	
#FFCCFF		#CCCCFF		#99CCFF	
#FFCCCC		#CCCCCC		#99CCCC	
#FFCC99		#CCCC99		#99CC99	
#FFCC66		#CCCC66		#99CC66	
#FFCC33		#CCCC33		#99CC33	
#FFCC00		#CCCC00		#99CC00	
#FF99FF		#CC99FF		#9999FF	
#FF99CC		#CC99CC		#9999CC	
#FF9999		#CC9999		#999999	
#FF9966		#CC9966		#999966	
#FF9933		#CC9933		#999933	

❷

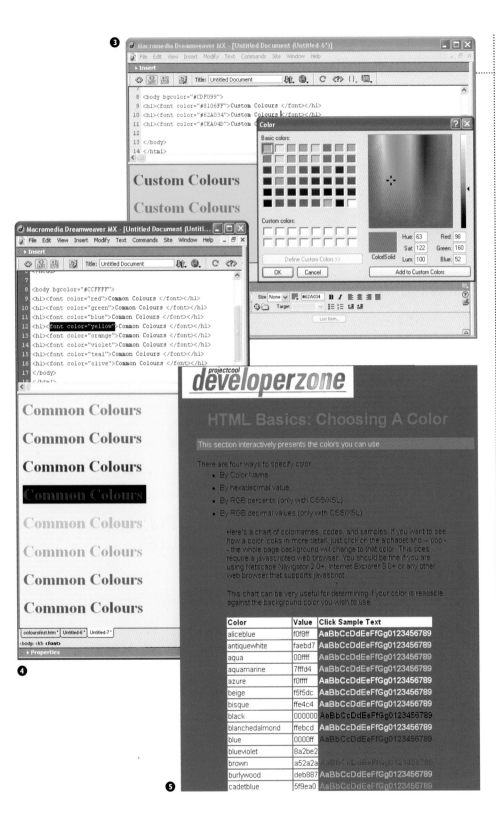

1 *The easiest way to specify type colors is to use the Web-safe colors available via the Properties panel. Dreamweaver automatically adds the necessary tag.*

2 *If you're entering code manually, check out a site like* **www.webmonkey.com**, *which provides a reference chart of Web-safe colors.*

3 *In fact, any of 16.7 million colors can be specified either directly or via a sub-dialog.*

4 *The most common colors can be specified by name from within your HTML code.*

5 *The developer zone at* **www.devx.com** *is particularly useful becauses it quickly lets you see how well any named color contrasts against another.*

PROJECT 7:
TYPE COLOR & SPACE

<Font color="…"> enables us to specify the color of our type, but it's not the only "color" that the typographer will bear in mind. One of the main characteristics of any typeface is its inherent personality—sometimes referred to, confusingly, as its "color." Some typefaces are more solid and heavy than others.

It's important to realize that it's not just the type itself that has color (by the usual definition). Just as the canvas is a crucial color element in a painting, so the page background is in graphic design. In fact, in many ways white space is the most important color of all (it's called "white" because this is the usual color of paper, but on the Web it can be any color we choose).

The simplest way to bring the background color fully into play is to vary the alignment of the paragraphs. HTML 3.2 offers the "align" attribute, which can be applied to block level tags such as <p> and <h1> for exactly this purpose. An opening <h1 align="right"> tag will right align the heading that follows it. The creative use of white space surrounding our text blocks breaks up the content and lets the design breathe, while at the same time opening up entry points and helping to indicate the hierarchy of importance in the content.

The expert type user will deliberately mix all these color and spacing options to offset each other. They can do so to create a dynamic balance, or sometimes an imbalance works better. Just as an artist works with different colors of paint, the typographer works with different colors of type.

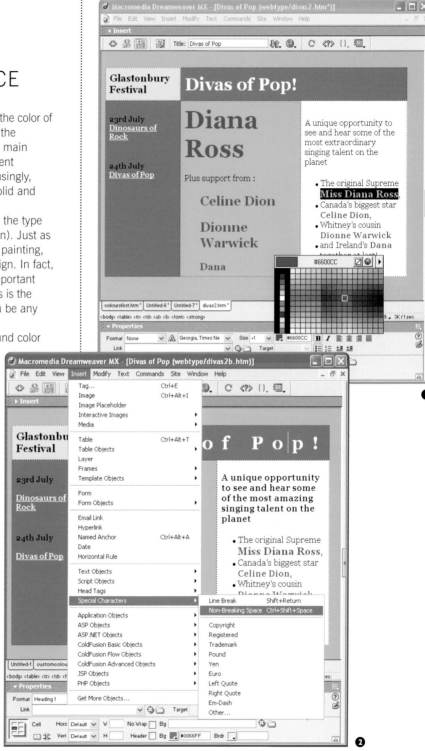

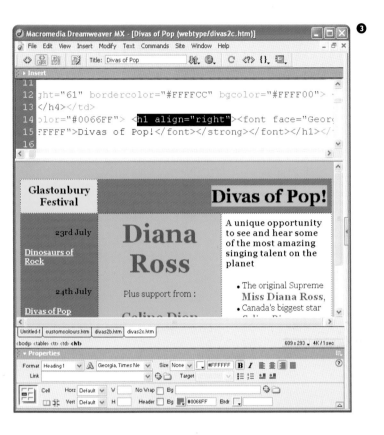

❸

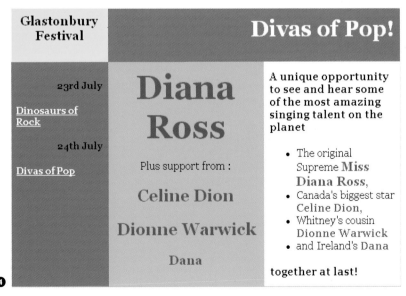

❹

❶ When applying colors to our festival page, it would be very easy to go over the top—especially considering the existing cell-based colors. However, by limiting ourselves to three type colors—black for the body copy, white for titles, and purple for the artists' names—we can pull out the elements we want highlighted. We can also reinforce the underlying information structure and add variety without distracting attention.

❷ We can also try and change the text's inherent color with some emboldening of paragraphs. Unfortunately, HTML doesn't provide control of interline, intercharacter, or interword spacing, so the nearest we can get is faking it. Add non-breaking spaces between characters, and line breaks to create space between paragraphs. Here, it just doesn't work, but it's worth a try!

❸ What we can do instead is to use the *Properties* panel to quickly apply left, right and center alignment, thus opening up our layout (full justification isn't an option with HTML 3.2). Dreamweaver automatically adds the necessary alignment attributes to the block-level tags.

❹ The end result is a much more colorful, open, and attractive layout, which will also be easier to read.

78 PROJECT 8:

DESIGNER HTML SHOWCASE 1

At last it feels like we're getting some reasonable design and type control. So let's take stock and put everything together to produce a typical fan site's discography.

❶ Our first job is to set up the layout grid. This time, we're going to produce a more advanced layout, so add a table with three columns and five rows. Again, set the width to 580 pixels, the padding to eight, and the border to zero.

❷ Now merge the cells to produce the grid layout shown.

❸ Add some text along the following lines. What we're creating are separate sections for links, for the banner title, for the album titles, for the track listing, for the band members, and for some body copy.

❹ Now let's format the page's text as a whole. We could use the <basefont> tag, but some browsers, including Netscape, fail to support this when text is in tables, so we're going to play safe by applying a font tag to all the table cells. We're going to use Verdana as the main body font because it's a sans serif face that has been specially optimized for onscreen use. And because it may not be installed on all users' systems, we'll apply the formatting as a font list that degrades down to the browser's default "sans."

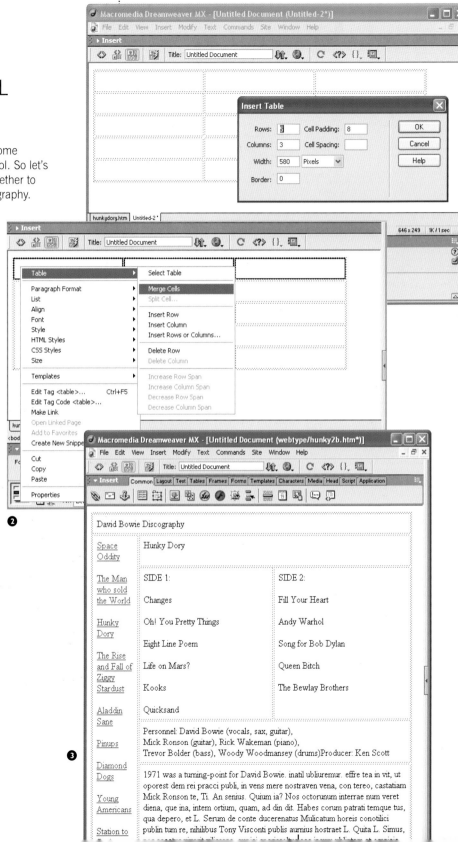

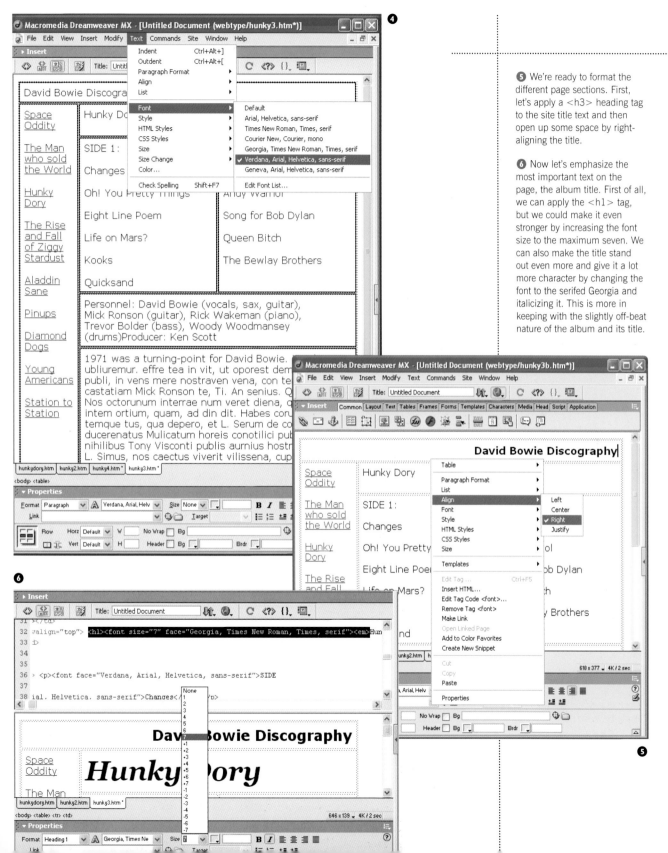

5 We're ready to format the different page sections. First, let's apply a <h3> heading tag to the site title text and then open up some space by right-aligning the title.

6 Now let's emphasize the most important text on the page, the album title. First of all, we can apply the <h1> tag, but we could make it even stronger by increasing the font size to the maximum seven. We can also make the title stand out even more and give it a lot more character by changing the font to the serifed Georgia and italicizing it. This is more in keeping with the slightly off-beat nature of the album and its title.

80

PROJECT 9:
DESIGNER HTML SHOWCASE 2

So far, so good. We've started to add some basic typographical features to this straightforward website design, but it's still not looking like a fully fledged site of the type you'll be familiar with from surfing the Web. So, how can we use some of the extended functionality of HTML 3.2 formatting to produce something that looks a little more professional and inviting to our prospective visitors? Remember, a site of this nature will be just one of many out there on the Internet: we want to create the site that people will look at in preference to all the others!

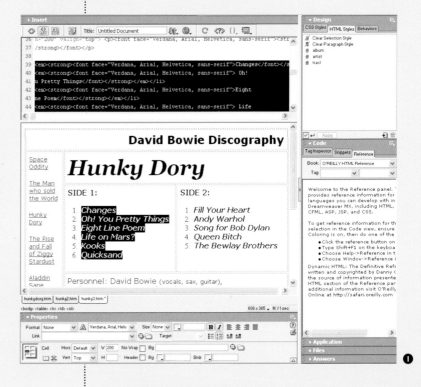

1 Let's move on to a two-column track list. Here we can make the type bold and then turn the italicized tracks into an <ol> ordered list so that they are automatically numbered. This is most easily done with the numbering shortcut on the *Properties* panel.

2 Next we can add some inline formatting. First we can use the <font size="-1"> tag to shrink the size of the album links proportionally, and the musical instrument text. We can also embolden text and add color to mark out the personnel involved. Doing this repeatedly would be a chore, so Dreamweaver makes it possible to set up a named HTML style that automatically applies multiple tags.

3 For the finishing touches, we can add some layout color. First of all, use the *Modify>Page Properties* command to set the overall background color to a Web-safe light cream. Next, use the *Properties* panel to select a choice of complementary orange and yellow colors to apply to the album title, album tracks, and band member cells. Set the body copy cell to white to maintain maximum type contrast.

4 Finally, we can preview the page in the two most common browsers, Netscape and Explorer, to check for problems. Thankfully, while the designs aren't identical, each looks acceptable—which is what really counts.

❸

Where we stand

We've certainly come a long way from the limitations of plain vanilla HTML. And it's this extended HTML 3.2 formatting that is the basis of the majority of sites out there on the Web today.

But let's not get too excited. Yes, we've got some layout control, but it's still not as flexible as DTP multi-column layouts. Yes, we've got some size control, but having just seven sizes means that it's rudimentary at best. Yes, we can specify fonts, but our choice is limited—and whether they actually appear is another matter. Yes, our color control is impressive, but this is undercut by the almost non-existent control over type spacing.

And ultimately, whatever design ideas we come up with, the final interpretation of our layout and typography still depends on the end user's browser set-up. To top it all, you can virtually guarantee that just when you think you've come up with a cracking design, you'll find that it doesn't work in one of the main browsers, and so is functionally useless. No wonder Web design is often compared to trying to sculpt jelly—with one hand tied behind your back!

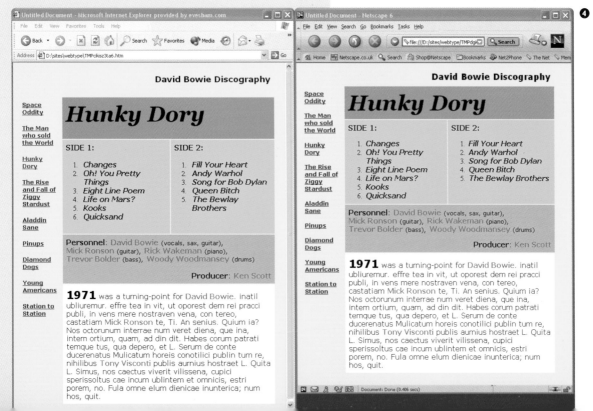

❹

WRITING
TYPOFILE
CHIPMUNKS
ESPERFONTO
TIME & TYPE

Web Sites
Logos
Cards
CDs
Book
Covers

GIF

WHO, ME?

FLASH TYPE

BALLET
DU NORD

BALLET
DU NORD

Bienvenue,
Pour ce site le plug-in Flash

O Vous avez Flash 5 - En

Bypassing HTML

The design-led HTML 3.2 extensions have given us much more typographic control than the core HTML 2 specification, but they are still basic when compared to the capabilities of DTP and image-editing programs, not to mention traditional typography. The question is: can we find some way to access some of that advanced design power for use on the Web?

Yes. We can work around HTML's limitations by using the Web to deliver other, more design-rich formats, such as the GIF image, the Flash SWF movie, or the Acrobat PDF publication.

Java

ype

ensable.

84 INTRODUCING BITMAP GIF IMAGES

By far the most common way to add advanced text-handling to your HTML webpage is to embed it as a bitmap image created in a design-rich application. A bitmap image is defined as a grid of colored pixels.

There are two common bitmap formats that are used on the Web: JPEG and GIF. JPEG (a format developed by the Joint Photographic Experts Group) is particularly well suited for handling continuous tone photographic images in which each pixel's color tends to be different to its neighbors. Common examples are images produced by a scanner or a digital camera. The other bitmap format, GIF (Graphics Interchange Format), is particularly well suited for images that contain areas of flat, repeating color, such as buttons and text.

GIF images have a number of advantages for type handling. All browsers support the format natively, and all Web-authoring applications make it simple to add images to your HTML-based page by using the <img> image tag. In terms of type handling, being able to control the image down to the individual pixel level means that any DTP-style typographical feature can be reproduced—along with a wide variety of added creative options, such as drop shadows and texture fills.

The big downside of GIF type compared to HTML type is that it's not just the character codes of the text that must be downloaded, but every pixel of every glyph. GIF offers excellent compression to make this as efficient as possible, but it's still bandwidth heavy, which means slow download times. In addition, the text in the GIF is no longer live, which means it can't be copied and pasted and search engines won't be able to add it to their databases.

Clearly, then, a GIF image isn't the right option for creating a whole site, or even a page of text, but it's perfect for adding a short title or headline that really stands out and brings your page to life.

1

2

3

Glastonbury Festival

Divas of Pop!

23rd July

Dinosaurs of Rock

24th July

Divas of Pop

Diana Ross

Plus support from :

Celine Dion

Dionne Warwick

Dana

A unique opportunity to see and hear some of the most amazing singing talent on the planet

- The original Supreme **Miss Diana Ross,**
- Canada's biggest star Celine Dion,
- Whitney's cousin Dionne Warwick
- and Ireland's **Dana**

together at last!

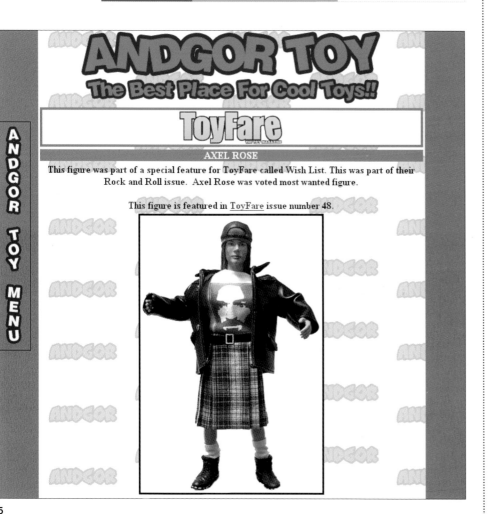

ANDGOR TOY
The Best Place For Cool Toys!!

ToyFare

ANDGOR TOY MENU

AXEL ROSE

This figure was part of a special feature for ToyFare called Wish List. This was part of their Rock and Roll issue. Axel Rose was voted most wanted figure.

This figure is featured in ToyFare issue number 48.

5

1 *Each bitmap image is built as a grid of colored pixels. Zoom in and you can see the individual pixels; zoom out and the eye sees the image as a whole. For type, handling, this means that we can use any typeface we like!*

2 *Their respective compression systems mean that the JPEG format is ideal for handling continuous-tone photographs, and the GIF format is good for handling images with areas of solid, flat color.*

3 *With its <img> image tag, HTML supports GIF and JPEG images directly, which means that any browser will be able to see your image and your type.*

4 *You could produce an entire Web page as a GIF, but the download size is much larger, you can't select any text or embed hyperlinks, and the text isn't searchable.*

5 *GIF type certainly isn't right for a whole page, but it can be perfect for headings with impact. Here the outlined and angled characters catch the eye and deliver the fun message.*

BITMAP AUTHORING APPS

To produce your bitmaps, you're going to need a bitmap authoring application. The main market for bitmap editors is in scanning and enhancing photos, so we're going to be looking at a range of photo editors. In particular, we're looking for a bitmap photo-editing application that is good at handling type and offers optimized output to the GIF format.

So which is the right package for you? If you include shareware applications, there are dozens of alternatives to choose from, but they tend to fall into three main camps.

The world of professional bitmap-editing is entirely dominated by one application: Adobe Photoshop. Photoshop began life long before the Internet, and its main focus is still on photo-editing destined for print. Over the last five years, however, it has also added serious type-handling and Web-oriented features for Web designers to get their teeth into.

The second group of bitmap editors is focussed entirely on producing bitmaps for use on the Web. As such, in addition to core photo-editing capabilities, these applications provide dedicated Web features, such as image slicing and rollover creation. Photoshop includes its own Web add-on, Image-Ready, but the dominant dedicated web image editor is Macromedia Fireworks.

The third group is of general consumer-oriented applications, such as Jasc Paint Shop Pro, Ulead PhotoImpact, Corel Photo-Paint, and the cut-down version of Adobe's killer app, Photoshop Elements. These are all aimed more at the digital camera user than the professional photographer but, while they don't offer the same high-end features as Photoshop/ImageReady or Fireworks, they all provide everything that you need to produce Web type and to output it to GIF format.

The bottom line is that almost all photo editors are capable these days of producing eye-catching and efficient Web type. Things are looking up!

1

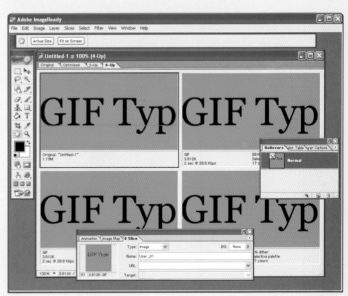

2

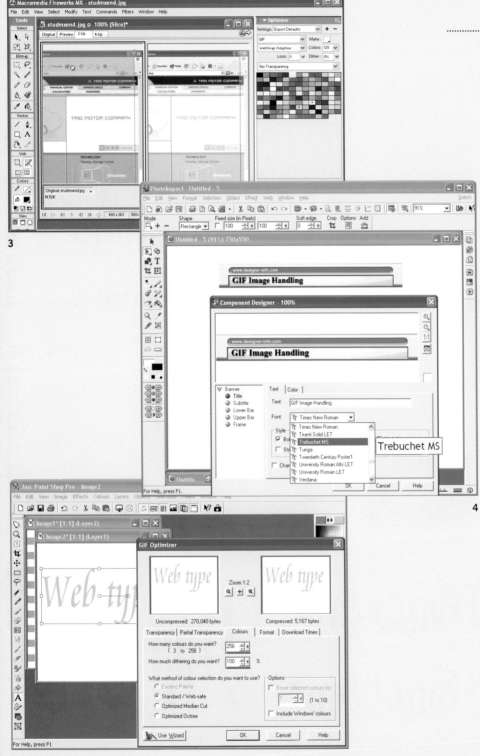

3

5

4

1 *With features such as CMYK support and channel handling, Photoshop is primarily aimed at professional print-oriented photo-editing.*

2 *Photoshop also now targets Web image-authoring and includes the dedicated ImageReady to provide features such as rollover production.*

3 *Macromedia Fireworks offers the most advanced Web image creation, optimization and integration. A common interface makes it the perfect graphical partner for Dreamweaver.*

4 *Some consumer image-editing applications, most notably Ulead PhotoImpact, provide Web features that put the professional tools to shame.*

5 *Even the budget Paint Shop Pro is able to handle type as vectors—this is particularly important, because it means that you can go back to your text later to re-edit it if you wish.*

88 PROJECT 10:
BITMAP TYPE-HANDLING 1

To see bitmap-based type-handling in action, we're going to use Photoshop Elements, as it offers almost all of the type-handling power of Photoshop at a fraction of the cost. And to show the advantages of the pixel-based approach to type at its best, we're going to produce a graphical logo for an up-and-coming heavy metal band. An uncomfortable mix of Black Sabbath, Kiss, and Marilyn Manson—welcome to the dark and dangerous world of "Trancystor"! Well, you never know; it could happen.

❶ Our first task is to take a look at what typefaces are available to us. Using the text tool and the *Property* bar, we can look for all faces with the right kind of feel—definitely old style, preferably slightly threatening, but with tongue firmly in cheek. Many of the body fonts have something going for them, but ultimately prove a little too dull, whereas some of the display type offerings are just too clichéd.

2 This is a one-off logo, so we want to get it right, and that means looking for the perfect font. Looking on the Web, there Is a great range of free fonts available from *www.autofx.com*. Under the Strange category, there's the ideal candidate, Parry Hotter, clearly inspired by the font used for the Harry Potter film and so providing just the right mix of mystery and menace—in a friendly sort of way, of course.

3 Once installed and applied to our text, the first impressions are positive—the capital T with its lightning stroke effect is particularly striking. Unfortunately, the central "y" is a bit weak, but we can overcome this by making it upper case and shrinking it proportionately. We can also give the logo greater weight and make it a bit more intimidating by stretching it vertically.

4 Thanks to the vector nature of the type, we can do more than just stretch it. Using the *Warp Text* command, we can experiment with a whole range of distortions. In the end, I chose the *Inflate* effect.

5 As we're going to output the image as pixels, the range of possible formatting is enormous. The *Layer Styles* palette provides plenty of bevels, glows, and textures to explore. For our logo, let's pull out all the stops with a two-tone chrome effect— very tasteful!

6 And to show off our pixel-level control, we're also going to add a strapline to the logo in one of those body copy fonts we looked at earlier. If the type is very small, remember that it's usually better to switch off the default antialiasing.

90   **PROJECT 11:**
BITMAP TYPE HANDLING 2

Designing our logo is only half of the story. Now we have to convert it from Photoshop Elements' own native PSD format into a GIF file that we can post to the Web. It's this GIF that our end users will actually see when they log onto our site.

❶ To do this, we need to get to grips with Photoshop Elements' dedicated *Save for Web* dialog, which shows previews of both our original image and of the final output image. The trick here is to get as low an output file size as possible (indicated under the preview) while maintaining acceptable onscreen quality.

We can start by exploring the presets. The first, "GIF 128 dither," produces a GIF export file size of almost 30k compared to the original PSD file of 469k. Swapping to "GIF 32 no dither" reduces this to just under 20k. In fact, we can cut it down even further by reducing the number of colors from 32 to eight. This does affect onscreen quality, but we can live with it, as it cuts the final output file size down to a much more acceptable 13k.

❷

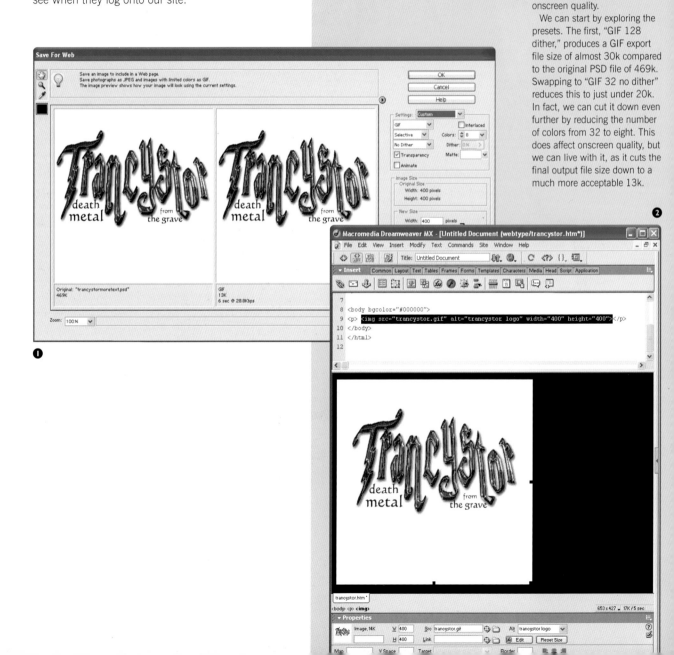

❶

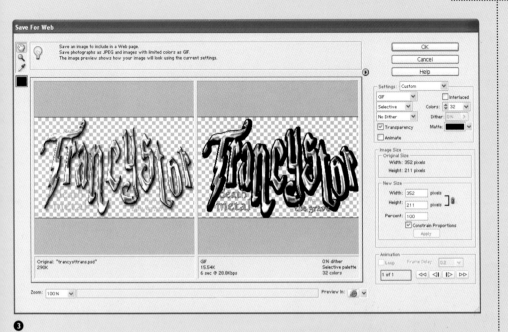

❸

❹

❷ Having saved our GIF, we're ready to insert it into Dreamweaver using the *Insert Image* command from the *Insert* toolbar. Dreamweaver automatically creates the <img> tag for us and we can add an alternative text description in the *Properties* panel in case visitors have turned off images in their browser preferences. We've got a problem, though. Any self-respecting website for this type of music is going to have a dark background, and the white surround to our image makes it look far too clean and friendly.

❸ In fact, it needn't be a problem because the GIF format supports transparency. If we go back to our original image, we can delete the background layer so that our text is left floating above a transparent background. While we're there, we can crop the image to make a tighter fit and change the text formatting to a style that will stand out better over black. Then, in the *Save for Web* dialog, we need to set the matt color to black—it's this color which Photoshop Elements uses to anti-alias the edges of the type.

❹ Now when we load this GIF, it looks good against any dark background (here we've used a textured pattern). To give the page as a whole more impact and consistency, we can also pick up on certain features of our bitmap type. There's virtually no chance of our end users having the unusual Parry Hotter font installed, but they might have the font we used for the strapline, so we can set this as the first option in our font list. We can also pick up on the strapline text's color to tie our HTML type and GIF logo together into a single coherent whole.

92 INSPIRATION:
WILL-HARRIS.COM

There are plenty of sites around that show exactly how effective the use of bitmapped type can be, but as a good example take *www.will-harris.com.* It's the home site for graphic designer Daniel Will-Harris, and it's an excellent showcase for his work. Daniel is a longstanding type expert who, among other claims to fame, has helped produce the templates that ship with CorelDraw, Corel Ventura and Microsoft Publisher. There's plenty of type-related material on the site and it's well worth visiting for information as well as inspiration.

1

1 *The first thing that hits you when you arrive at the site's home page is the graphical use of bitmapped type. The main font is particularly striking. It's very heavy and monumental and set all in uppercase, but this is undercut by oddities such as the fluid S and R that make the font seem either hand-drawn or produced with Letraset—a feeling reinforced by the way that the letters have been set so closely on a tight grid. The central message is clear: we have arrived at a design-intensive and design-oriented site.*

2

5

3

4

DESIGN OFFICE

Please take a look at my designs. I'm available for work no matter where in the world you are. If you're interested in having me work for you, just drop me a note.

WEB

State of the art sites. See more...

FLASH

Flash Animation (and more)

LOGOS

As a designer, I believe that logos are powerful symbols that help establish an *identity* for your company, group, or product. As a person I also think they're *a lot of fun.* It's a challenge to create a visual personality based on a company's or product's personality. It's a weird, graphic form of portraiture, and it uses a great deal of symbolism, and knowledge of the psychology of forms and colors. Come take a look...

PACKAGES

Package Designs, Software boxes, software CD covers, and a poster for a play.

Music CD - See my latest music cd package, a laid-back design including cover, back, inside cover and cd itself.

CARDS

- Business Card Designs: Nine unique cards for seven unique women.
- More Card Designs: Seven cards and a fold-out.

6

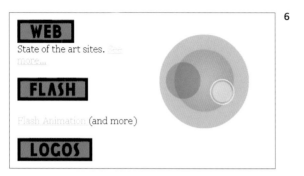

7

3|4|5 *To begin with, Will-Harris has translated the home page's graphical type into a smaller but still extremely strong rollover-based navigational device.*

6 *He's also picked up the same font to use for image headings in the text. It's recognizably the same typeface, but Will-Harris has made the headings stand out with a strongly contrasting blue background. He's also spaced out the letters of the text and given them a wide surrounding margin to ensure that this use of the heading font is both eye-catching and highly legible.*

7 *For his body copy, Will-Harris has picked Georgia: a sensible choice because its serifs are reminiscent of hand-drawn type, so in keeping with the site's feel. Will-Harris has also used a table layout to restrict the line length of his text, keeping it more readable, and used his signature typeface to create a logo based on his initials. A subtle version is used as a background pattern.*

8 *Inspect the underlying code and you can see exactly how the site has been put together. Although they are largely based on bitmaps, the home page and navigation device have actually been created as Flash movies (see the next pages). The blue headings, meanwhile, are all handled as separate GIFs while the HTML body copy is formatted with extensive use of the <font> tag and font lists. Some sensible use of CSS would have made life a lot easier, but this site isn't about easy: it's about impact.*

```
design[1] - Notepad
File  Edit  Format  View  Help
HREF="./design/flash.html"><FONT FACE="Georgia, Verdana, Trebuchet, Times New
Roman, Times"></FONT></A><A HREF="./design/logos.htm"><IMG
ID="Picture1503" HEIGHT=37 WIDTH=20 SRC="./design/o.gif" VSPACE=0 HSPACE=0
ALIGN="BOTTOM" BORDER=0></A><A HREF="./design/flash.html"><FONT
FACE="Georgia, Verdana, Trebuchet, Times New Roman, Times"></FONT></A><A
HREF="./design/logos.htm"><IMG ID="Picture1504" HEIGHT=37 WIDTH=18
SRC="./design/g.gif" VSPACE=0 HSPACE=0 ALIGN="BOTTOM" BORDER=0></A><A
HREF="./design/flash.html"><FONT FACE="Georgia, Verdana, Trebuchet, Times New
Roman, Times"></FONT></A><A HREF="./design/logos.htm"><IMG
ID="Picture1505" HEIGHT=37 WIDTH=20 SRC="./design/o.gif" VSPACE=0 HSPACE=0
ALIGN="BOTTOM" BORDER=0></A><A HREF="./design/flash.html"><FONT
FACE="Georgia, Verdana, Trebuchet, Times New Roman, Times"></FONT></A><A
HREF="./design/logos.htm"><IMG ID="Picture1508" HEIGHT=37 WIDTH=12
SRC="./design/s.gif" VSPACE=0 HSPACE=0 ALIGN="BOTTOM" BORDER=0></A><A
HREF="./design/flash.html"><FONT FACE="Georgia, Verdana, Trebuchet, Times New
Roman, Times"></FONT></A><A HREF="./design/logos.htm"><IMG
ID="Picture1506" HEIGHT=37 WIDTH=20 SRC="./design/rr.gif" VSPACE=0 HSPACE=0
ALIGN="BOTTOM" BORDER=0></A><A HREF="./design/flash.html"><FONT
FACE="Georgia, Verdana, Trebuchet, Times New Roman, Times"></FONT><FONT
FACE="Georgia, Verdana, Trebuchet, Times New Roman, Times"> <P>As a
designer, I believe that  logos are powerful symbols that help establish
an <I>identity</I> for your company, group, or product. As a person I 
also think they're <I>a lot of fun.</I>
It's a challenge to  create a visual personality based on a company's
or  product's personality. It's a weird, graphic form of 
portraiture, and it uses a great deal of symbolism, and  knowledge of
the psychology of forms and colors. </FONT><A HREF="./design/logos.htm"><FONT
FACE="Georgia, Verdana, Trebuchet, Times New Roman, Times">Come take a
look...</FONT></A><FONT FACE="Georgia, Verdana, Trebuchet, Times New Roman,
Times"><P><A HREF="./design/software-cd.htm"><IMG
ID="Picture1509" HEIGHT=37 WIDTH=20 SRC="./design/ll.gif" VSPACE=0 HSPACE=0
ALIGN="BOTTOM" BORDER=0></A><A HREF="./design/software-cd.htm"><IMG
ID="Picture1510" HEIGHT=37 WIDTH=16 SRC="./design/p.gif" VSPACE=0 HSPACE=0
ALIGN="BOTTOM" BORDER=0></A><A HREF="./design/software-cd.htm"><IMG
```

8

94 INTRODUCING FLASH SWF MOVIES

Using a bitmap GIF is the most common way of adding a type-based image to your webpage, but that doesn't necessarily mean it's the best way. In particulars the need to send every single pixel is inherently bandwidth-heavy and wasteful.

A much more efficient system is to send the glyphs as mathematical descriptions, or "vectors," especially as this means that the same image can be used at any size with no loss of quality. This is exactly what the Macromedia Flash SWF (Shockwave Flash format) format does.

The problem is that, unlike GIF, none of the browsers support the SWF format natively. Fortunately, this isn't too much of a problem any more because Macromedia makes its Flash player plug-in available from its website and this also comes bundled with most browsers. The end result is that Macromedia claims that over 98% of users should be able to see any Flash content that you post on your site.

The reason that over 500 million users have downloaded the player isn't just because of Flash's vector efficiency. Flash has plenty of other advantages. In particular, Flash doesn't just offer static images—it's a dynamic medium. At its simplest, this means the ability to produce animations, but Flash also lets expert users incorporate audio, video, and advanced interactivity to create a rich multimedia experience. Best of all, it manages to provide all of this power so efficiently that the results can even be delivered over a standard dial-up modem connection.

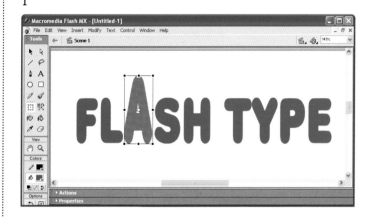

1

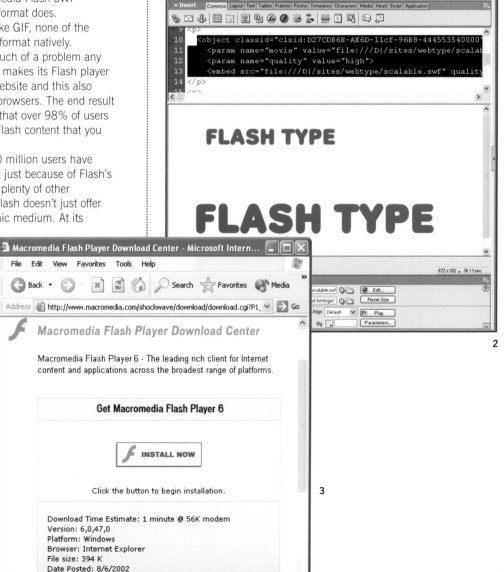

2

3

4

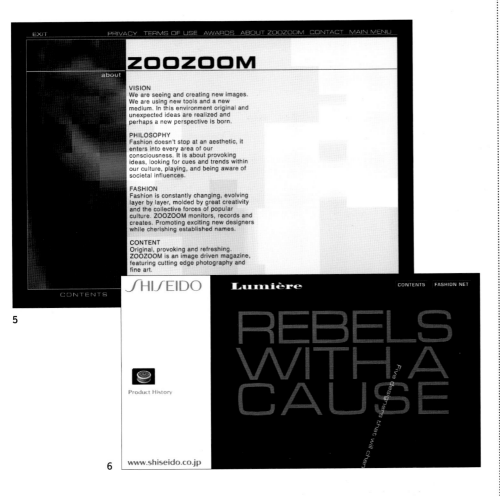

1 *Type in Flash is handled as scalable and efficient mathematical vectors rather than as a collection of download-heavy pixels.*

2 *Adding a Flash file to your webpage isn't as simple as with the GIF's <img> tag, but it's made easier in a dedicated package like Dreamweaver. This takes care of the coding for you. Once imported, you can resize your image interactively.*

3 *Any user can download the Flash player from* www.macromedia.com.

4 *Although we're going to be concentrating on Flash's type handling, this is only a fraction of the power that Flash offers. It's actually the features such as audio and video support and programmatic control that are the real secret of Flash's popularity. That's why Flash calls its SWF files "movies."*

5|6 *Webites such as* www.zoozoom.com *and* www.lumiere.com *show just what Flash can do with a mix of simple type, pictures, sound, and interactivity.*

5

6

96

FLASH AUTHORING APPS

Flash is an amazing technology. At its simplest, it lets you produce efficient and dynamic text, buttons, and banners that help bring your HTML webpages to life. At its most advanced, it enables you to produce self-contained, scalable, interactive, multimedia extravaganzas that replace HTML entirely and operate just like a local application on your own system, even though they are being delivered over the Web.

So what's the best way to go about producing your Flash files?

The most obvious route to choose is Macromedia's own authoring application, Flash MX. This is really the only way to produce the most advanced Flash work since it requires the ability to control interactivity with Flash's own programing language, ActionScript. That's outside the scope of this book (see its sister-title, *Web Expert: Animation* for information), but there are other ways of producing dynamic Flash type.

These days, all of the major drawing applications including—Adobe Illustrator, Corel Draw, Macromedia FreeHand and Deneba Canvas—offer the ability to export to SWF format and to map layers to frames, producing simple flick-book style Flash animations.

Other packages provide dedicated Flash authoring. Corel R.A.V.E. (included in the Corel Draw suite) and Adobe LiveMotion both offer timeline-based editing, basic control over interactivity, and the ability to produce dynamic files that have considerable impact.

There are also a number of smaller utility programs, often in the form of shareware, that take advantage of SWF. Of these, by far the best for type-based animation is SWiSH, which takes an effect-based approach to provide maximum impact at minimum cost.

If you use Dreamweaver MX, you can even add the occasional static Flash headline or rollover button directly from within the program. In-depth reviews of all these applications are available at *www.designer-info.com*, among others.

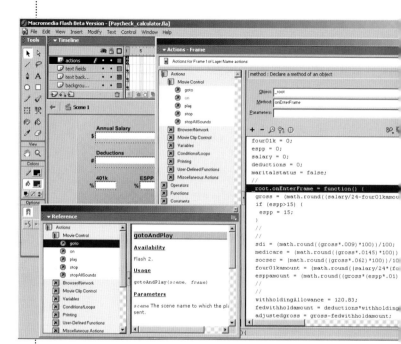

1

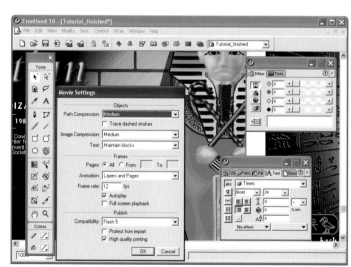

2

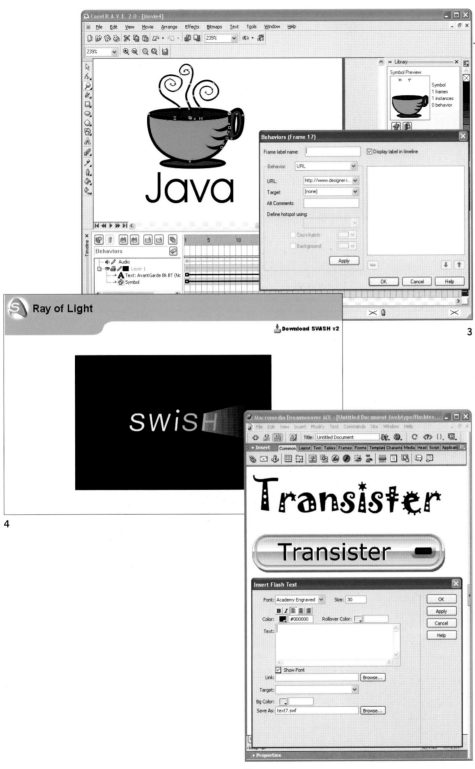

1 *By far the most powerful Flash authoring solution is Macromedia's own Flash MX application—although at times it can seem more like an entire programming environment than design software.*

2 *It's no surprise that the drawing program which emphasizes its Flash output and integration more than any other is Macromedia's own FreeHand application.*

3 *Corel Draw offers export to SWF format and a dedicated Flash authoring add-on, Corel R.A.V.E. (standing for "Real Animation Video Effects").*

4 *You can download the excellent SWiSH from www.swishzone.com. It majors on type-handling and eye-catching effects, which are ideal for our purposes, but it also offers real drawing and animation power.*

5 *Dreamweaver MX's Insert> Interactive Images>Flash Text command lets you add simple sections of Web type in any font installed on your system. Using the Flash Button option, you can also turn your text into interactive rollover buttons.*

98 PROJECT 12:
FLASH TYPE-HANDLING 1

So let's explore what the Flash SWF format has to offer. As the full Macromedia Flash MX application would be serious overkill for our needs, we're going to save ourselves time, effort, and money by using the excellent SWiSH (available from *www.swishzone.com*).

To give both the SWF format and SWiSH application a good workout, we're going to produce another band logo. But this time we're going to the other extreme of the musical spectrum, producing an identity for a modernist, androgynous dance outfit. A self-confident cross between Kraftwerk and Fischerspooner. Welcome to the world of "Transister."

❶

❷

❸

❶ The first step, as always, is to explore what typefaces we have available to us. This time, we're looking at sans serif faces, especially those with a clearly futuristic feel.

❷ To highlight the androgynous nature of the band, we're going to make play of the central pun by using different typefaces for "tran" and "sister." This instantly adds interest and it also gives us the opportunity to balance different weights of typeface and color to produce an internal creative dynamic. Choosing a strong, almost industrial typeface for the word "sister" is a design pun, and the heavy text can be brought back into balance by using a lighter blue.

❸ We still want to make the logo more graphical. The central role of the pivotal "s" provides the perfect opportunity. One of the advantages of Flash's vector technology is that we can easily edit the default type, stretching and squashing it and, by converting the letters to curves, even edit the glyph shapes. Ultimately, though, we decided these tricks were too over the top for a minimalist band and instead chose to recolor the "s" as a dark blue, so that it acts as a bridge between both sections of type.

❹ As with the GIF logo, we can also add a strapline. Again, it's a good idea to choose a contrasting but complementary typeface. Tahoma makes a good choice. It has a particularly strong, bold version, and is a common Web typeface, so we'll be able to pick up on it in the rest of the page.

❹

100

PROJECT 13:
FLASH TYPE-HANDLING 2

If we now export our logo, we can already see two key advantages of SWF vector handling: a file size of just 4k, and the ability to resize our text to any size we desire without any loss of image quality. Try doing the same with a GIF image and the quality will noticeably degrade.

The real advantage of the Flash format, however, is that we can now use animation to bring our type to life.

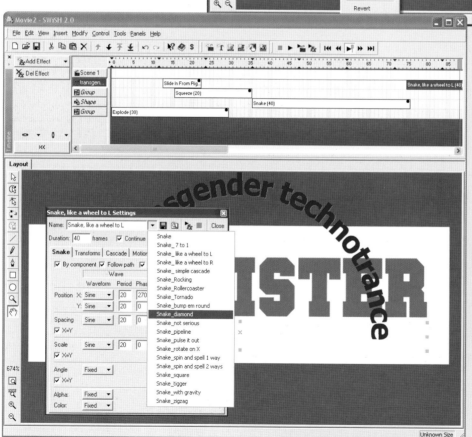

❶ In the SWiSH Timeline above the central drawing area, you will see that each of our four type objects has automatically been added on its own layer. To add an animation effect, select the object or layer and then click the *Insert >Effect* command. Choose from one of the broad effect categories that appear.

❷ Within each category, SWiSH offers plenty of presets from the dropdown list at the top of the dialog. You can also fine-tune each effect in the different tabs of the dialog. Preview the effect with the *Play* command at the top right of the dialog. Click *Close* to apply the effect and it appears as a named bar on the Timeline. You can reposition and drag the bars to control what happens when, and for how long. You can double-click on the bar to re-edit the animation settings.

③ The best way to see the possibilities on offer is to explore—just have fun mixing up multiple effects and see which ones work best. You'll soon find out that the range of effects on offer is extraordinary, ranging from simple Fade-Ins and Outs to advanced effects like *Explode*, which makes it look like a bomb has gone off under your type. Trying to produce the same sort of effects in Flash MX might actually take days of effort.

④ Some of these advanced effects will certainly catch your audience's attention, but again they are a bit over the top for the minimalist feel we are aiming for. In the end, we've gone for two relatively simple animations. The first is the "Transform, grow thin and back" preset applied to the strapline, which stretches alternate letters and has a "rave" feel to it. We want the main "Transister" type to be readable onscreen at all times, so here we've set up a simple spin effect so that the pivotal "s" rotates. We've also fine-tuned and repeated the effect so that the color changes as the letter rotates between the black and the light blue. After one revolution the "s" seems more part of "trans" and after the next it is appears as part of "sister."

⑤ We're now ready to export our movie from SWiSH (the final size is still just 6k) and import it into Dreamweaver to produce the overall page. Notice how the strapline's Tahoma is picked up for the main font. The results are certainly eye-catching and we're able to notch up a major benefit for Web typography— after all, you can't animate paper-based type.

102 **INSPIRATION:**
BALLET DU NORD

Using Flash for any sort of type-handling can be a risky business—without a clear design idea and some self control, the results can be ugly or self-indulgent. As an example of how to do it, point your browser toward www.balletdunord.com. It's the home page for the French company Le Ballet du Nord and the site was produced by ATYPICLAB, a French web design company specializing in Flash. The thinking behind the site is clear—a modern ballet company needs an exciting dynamic design.

2

3

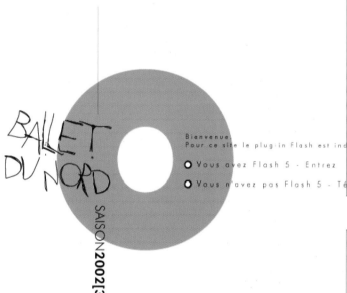

1

4

The shift to this heavy regular type is a striking change, but the two irregular horizontal lines still connect us back to the dynamic intro.

6 Gradually the screen fills in with more stick-like ballet figures and the central photo, but what catches the eye the most is still the type-handling. The Ballet Du Nord logo is redrawn onscreen and keeps oscillating slightly even when the rest of the page is still. At the same time the main content links appear. At first it looks as if something has gone wrong here as only the tops of the words appear. In fact this half-hidden effect is very deliberate. The text is still legible but the effect makes you more aware of the type's underlying graphical and line-based nature. And when you move your mouse over the link, the full word appears. The result is both dynamic and inviting.

7 The same device of half hiding the link text is used on many of the site's content pages. There isn't much body copy on any of the content pages which is just as well because what is there isn't amazingly readable. It's very small and not helped by Flash's automatic anti-aliasing.

Ultimately though www.balletdunord.com isn't about easy readability. In fact the use of Flash would be disastrous for both end users and authors alike if the site was intended to provide regular users with reams of content. What the site does instead is give the occasional visitor a strong flavour of the company itself—dynamic, modern, thought-provoking and above all imaginative. And its inspired use of type is central to achieving this goal.

1 The home page is simple and type-driven, showcasing four different kinds of text-handling. The most obvious is the logo for the company itself. In other circumstances, the hand-written text could look ugly, but here is's both modern and provocative. Next to it is the understated main block of text; below is the page title in an ultra modern font, set at right angles; and behind is the single capital O, which, as the only color on the page, invites the end user to click.

2|3|4 The introductory movie is a tour de force. Accompanied by music, a series of squiggles begin crossing the screen and then start resolving themselves into the sticklike ballet dancers and logo. Through animation, the type is brought alive as part of the dance.

5 After the intro we're through to the main welcome page. Again, type is used creatively with the message, "bienvenue," appearing in a solid bold black font laid over and balanced against a huge capital B that has been faded almost to white.

¹⁰⁴ INTRODUCING ACROBAT PDF PUBLICATIONS

Both GIF and Flash SWF have amazing strengths for creating static and dynamic type, but they are both suited only to adding short sections of text to your HTML pages. Neither of them can claim to offer true DTP-style typographic power for creating whole pages. Why can't we just have an electronic equivalent to paper?

This is exactly what Adobe's Acrobat PDF (Portable Document Format) provides. Based on its PostScript technology, Acrobat lets you create any possible print-oriented DTP-style page layout—with any typeface and typographical features, any graphics, and any color—in whatever application you choose and then output the results to a PDF file rather than to paper. Using Adobe's free Acrobat Reader program, your end user can then view the PDF document onscreen or print it out.

As with Macromedia's Flash player, you can be confident these days that the vast majority of your end users will have the Acrobat Reader, and so be able to view any PDFs that you post to your site. And thanks to PostScript's vector-based nature, the download sizes are reasonable and the text remains live—and therefore selectable and indexable by most search engines. Other strengths include the ability to add hyperlinks, multimedia elements, and basic interactivity, and to view PDFs directly within your browser.

This sounds like the Holy Grail of true "Web DTP." So why is HTML the language of the Web rather than PDF? It's partly a matter of HTML getting there first as well as being more open, universal, and extensible. The main reason, though, is fundamental. Acrobat's standalone and page-based nature is perfect for print but much less convenient or pleasurable for viewing onscreen.

Acrobat isn't a serious rival to HTML— but it is the perfect design-rich partner.

1

2

1 *The success of PDF is built on its PostScript foundations (seen here in WordPad). It's this underlying PostScript code that enables a PDF to include any embedded font.*

2 *Acrobat also wouldn't be a success without the free Reader program. It's this that enables the PDF to be viewed onscreen and printed to any device. Most users will already have the Reader installed. If not, you can get the latest version from* **www.adobe.com**.

3 *Originally intended for direct exchange, Acrobat files are now viewable directly in the Web browser. And thanks to the format's support for hypertext links, the PDF can act as an impressive cross between paper and webpage.*

4 *Effectively, Acrobat lets you produce full-color, design-intensive publications instantly, and at virtually no cost.*

5 *While PDFs have huge advantages, they also have drawbacks. In particular, trying to view and read a print-oriented page onscreen can sometimes be difficult. This is especially the case with large pages and multi-column layouts, and also where the typefaces used don't translate well to the screen.*

106 ACROBAT AUTHORING APPS

So what do you need to produce your Acrobat PDFs? Not surprisingly, Adobe, as the creator of the format, pushes its own applications' PDF capabilities heavily, but the format is an open standard and you have plenty of choice.

Most of the main professional drawing applications—CorelDraw, Adobe Illustrator, Macromedia FreeHand, and Deneba Canvas—provide direct export to PDF, while each of Adobe's DTP applications—InDesign, PageMaker, and FrameMaker—also offer good support. In fact, PDF is doubly useful for designers because, as well as providing the perfect electronic publishing format for posting to the Web, PDFs also act as the perfect digital master exchange medium for reliably producing commercial color-separated print.

But you don't need to buy one of these expensive authoring programs because you can produce PDF versions of any page layout produced with any application on any platform! The best way to do this is with Adobe's Acrobat application (don't confuse this with the free Reader utility). The full Acrobat suite includes a program called Distiller, which can take any PostScript print-to-disk file and convert it into a PDF. The Acrobat program also offers the ability to add multimedia, interactivity, annotations, and indexing, as well as to convert scanned pages to PDF.

If you don't need Acrobat's extended feature set, you can even produce your PDF files for free. PDF-Creator and GhostScript are freeware/shareware options that provide basic PDF authoring tools.

Once you've created your PDF file, you simply need to post it to your server and link to it from an HTML page. Assuming the end user has the Acrobat Reader program installed, this will open up the PDF within their browser application.

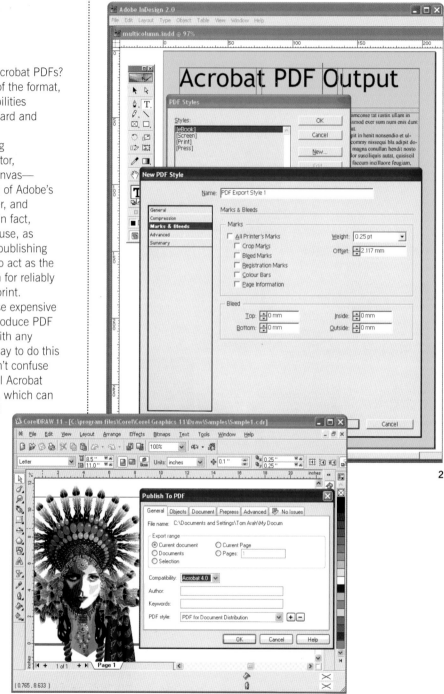

1

2

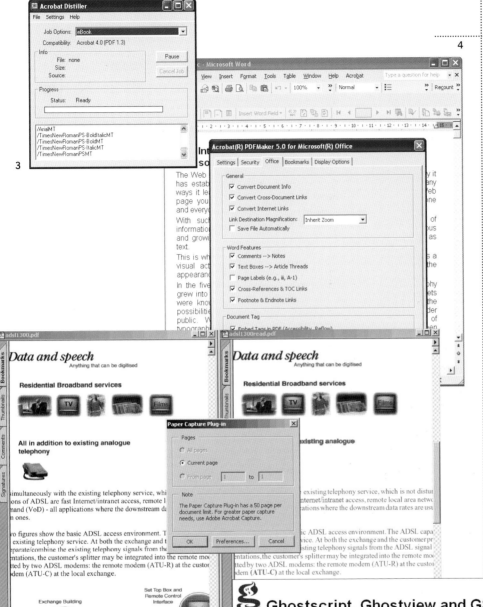

4

1 *All of the major design apps, such as CorelDraw, let you convert your designs to PDF.*

2 *InDesign has a particularly close tie-in to Acrobat—in fact, at one stage PDF was intended to be its native file format.*

3 *Acrobat 5's Distiller utility can convert any PostScript file to PDF format.*

4 *Acrobat also comes with dedicated support for Microsoft Office applications such as Word, so that features such as embedded links are automatically maintained.*

5 *Acrobat 5 also offers basic Paper Capture so that you can scan in existing pages, convert them to PDF, and then post them to the Web.*

6 *Shareware options available on the Web, such as Ghostscript/view, mean that you can produce basic PDFs for free. Point your browser towards http://www.cs.wisc.edu/~ghost for more detais and downloads.*

108

PROJECT 14:
PDF TYPE-HANDLING 1

When deciding what application to use to create our sample PDF, we're spoilt for choice—we could literally use any package. We're going to use PageMaker as an example, because it offers good DTP power at a reasonable price and lets us explore the two major ways of outputting to PDF.

Now that we've moved away from pure Web design, we're spoilt for typographic control. After the constraints and limitations of handling type in and with HTML, the gloves are off and we can really go to town. We're going to produce a typical print-oriented brochure of forthcoming events for a concert venue.

But despite its "print" appearance, we're going to pay attention to the need to read it onscreen. And, of course, the principles of good typography apply equally in either environment—as we've learned.

1 The first thing to do is to set up the page layout. Our design must work in print as well as on-screen, so we're going to produce a typical folded brochure. As it will be double-sided, I'll set the master page to two columns, then add four pages.

2 Then it's a case of bringing in the text to see the amount of copy we've got to deal with, and distributing it through the brochure page by page. We've then got to set up a main body copy style, which will set the tone for the brochure as a whole. As the main output will be to print, we've chosen Optima, which is a modern sans serif based on classical Roman writing. Because there's a lot of copy to fit in, set the body size to 9 point with 11 point interline spacing.

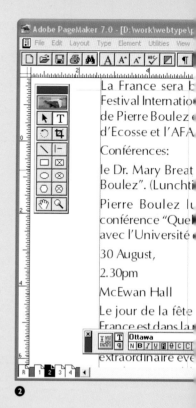

2

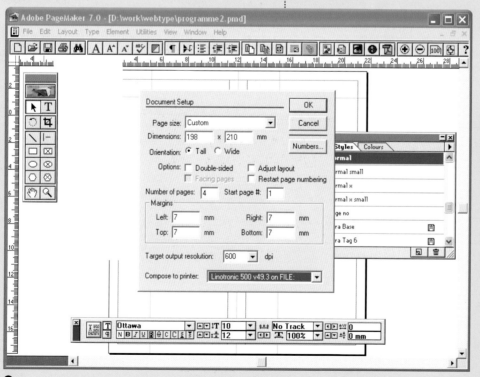

1

3 Now it's time to add some typographical order and interest. To mark out the headings, we've chosen Gill Sans Condensed, a clean modern typeface that works well in bold. We've also set up a wide side-margin, which gives the layout a feeling of space and luxury and can also be used to pick out date and venue details. Some strong bullets, inline emboldening, and ruling lines, and our type is soon easy to read, well-ordered—and inviting.

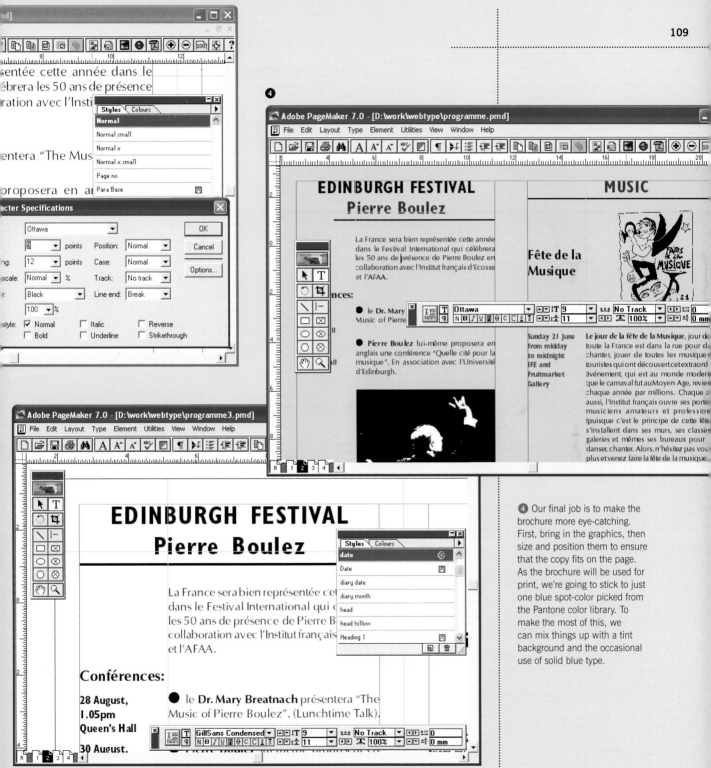

4 Our final job is to make the brochure more eye-catching. First, bring in the graphics, then size and position them to ensure that the copy fits on the page. As the brochure will be used for print, we're going to stick to just one blue spot-color picked from the Pantone color library. To make the most of this, we can mix things up with a tint background and the occasional use of solid blue type.

110   PROJECT 15:
PDF TYPE-HANDLING 2

Thanks to PageMaker's type-handling power, we've created a good, high-impact layout that we can send off for commercial print so that copies can be distributed locally around the venue. We want to attract the maximum possible audience, however, so we also need to make the brochure available over the Web. As we've examined, the PDF format is ideal for publishing to both destinations, and since PageMaker offers both in-built export and a bundled version of the Acrobat Distiller application, this gives us the perfect opportunity to explore the two most common means of creating PDFs.

❶

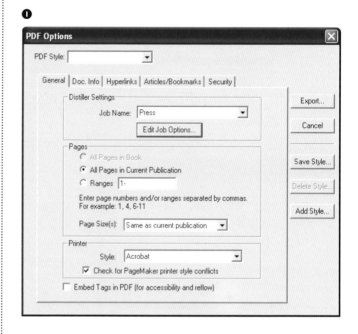

❷

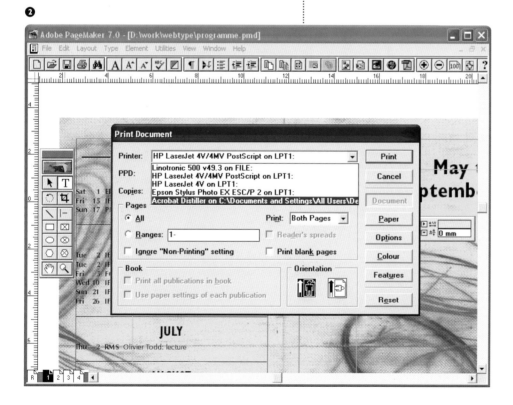

❶ The direct way is very simple. You simply select PageMaker's *File>Export> Adobe PDF* command and a dialog appears in which you can make the most common settings. In this case, we want our file to be ready to be output from our print bureau, so we need to set the Distiller *Job Settings* output to *Press*. Notice the other tabs in which you can control features such as hyperlinks, security, and so on. Once output, you can take the PDF to an output bureau ready for commercial print.

❸

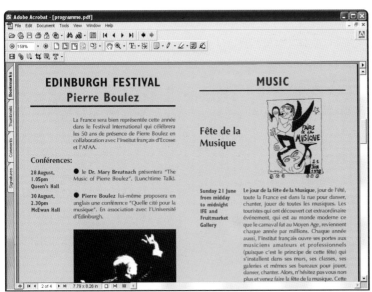

❷ That's fine for those applications that have direct export built-in. If we'd produced the layout in another program, say Word, we could still produce the PDF using Adobe's dedicated Acrobat program. This comes with a utility, Distiller, which automatically converts PostScript print files to PDF. To make this as simple as possible, Adobe installs the Distiller utility as if it was a printer, so that you can output your PDFs from your application's usual *Print* dialog.

❸ To control how Distiller creates the PDF, you need to open the application. For Web output, we need to set the main *Job Options* parameter to *Screen*. This will set up image compression and font handling designed to keep file sizes down (and therefore well suited to swift downloads). Using the *Edit>Job Options* command, you can also check that the *Compatibility* parameter is set to Acrobat 3.0 format to make sure the file is viewable by the maximum possible audience. Also ensure that Optimization is selected to enable the fastest possible Web viewing.

❹ Here's the end result opened for viewing in Acrobat. Notice how all the fonts and graphics are embedded in an exact electronic replica of the printed page. The design-intensive four-page PDF brochure with multiple photos is still under 100k in size. Simply by posting it to the server, it can be made instantly available to any Web user for onscreen reading and local printing.

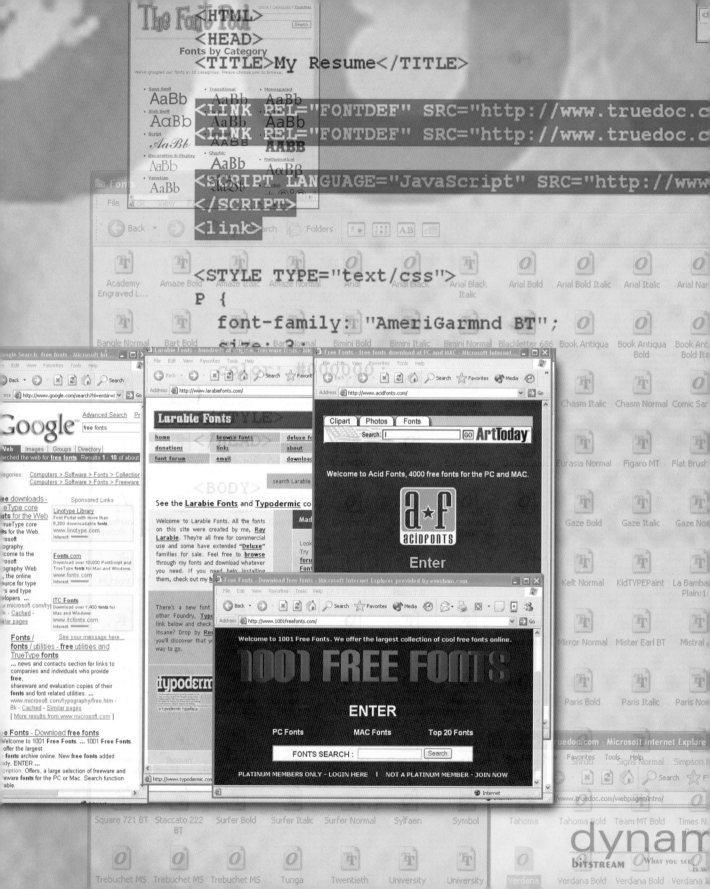

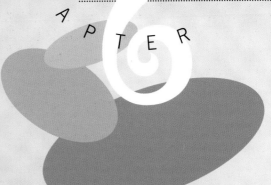

CHAPTER 6

Knowing and providing fonts

All of the major alternatives to HTML— GIF, SWF, and PDF—have an important part to play in the Web expert's armory, because they let you use any typeface that you want, with quite reliable results.

Ultimately, however, there's no getting away from the fact that the Web is built on HTML. This means that we have to make the most of the typography that HTML enables—and this means knowing what typefaces can safely be used with HTML.

If you want typography to become as powerful a tool on the Web as it is for print, you need some way to widen your choice of fonts. This is where "embedding" comes into play.

THE WEB FONT STANDARDS

Each webpage is built on HTML code, and this as we've seen, is a simple, ASCII text-only format. This means that unlike binary formats, such as SWF and PDF, we can't include scalable font information in the page itself. We can specify any font we want with the <font face="…"> tag, but, if the end user doesn't it have installed on their system, it simply won't appear. This much we know.

For body copy fonts, there's the extra complication that the face must be readable even when it's produced with spidery one-pixel wide strokes. Only a few typefaces have been specially designed for such low-resolution display: Times New Roman and Arial, their Mac equivalents, Times and Helvetica; and the newer Georgia, Verdana, and Trebuchet. You can also specify the fixed-pitch Courier if you don't mind your website looking like it was designed on a typewriter. Because these faces are provided with their respective operating systems, you can be reasonably confident that your end users will have them installed and that, if you specify them, this is what your end users will see.

For display type such as headings, we don't have the same low-resolution constraints and the choice of fonts is therefore wider. Theoretically, we can specify any font we want, but this makes sense only if a large proportion of the potential audience is likely to have the font installed. As Windows is by far the most popular operating system, and Internet Explorer is by far the most popular browser, you can be confident that the majority of your site visitors will also have the following display Web standards installed—Arial Black, Impact, and, for a more informal humorous look, Comic Sans MS.

There's nothing to stop you specifying any of these fonts, or any other, if you think it makes a real difference to your page. Crucially, though, remember to specify them with a font list so that if your first choice isn't available, your second will kick in.

1

Here is some text in all of the core web body fonts in this case **Arial** - see which you are comfortable reading and which suits the overall feel of your site. Also remember to check it out at various sizes.

Here is some text in all of the core web body fonts in this case **Times New Roman**- see which you are comfortable reading and which suits the overall feel of your site. Also remember to check it out at various sizes.

Here is some text in all of the core web body fonts in this case **Georgia** - see which you are comfortable reading and which suits the overall feel of your site. Also remember to check it out at various sizes.

Here is some text in all of the core web body fonts in this case **Verdana** - see which you are comfortable reading and which suits the overall feel of your site. Also remember to check it out at various sizes.

Here is some text in all of the core web body fonts in this case **Trebuchet** - see which you are comfortable reading and which suits the overall feel of your site. Also remember to check it out at various sizes.

Trebuchet MS, **Trebuchet MS Bold**, *Trebuchet MS Italic*, ***Bold Italic***

Trebuchet MS, designed by Vincent Connare in 1996, is a humanist sans serif designed for easy screen readability. Trebuchet takes its inspiration from the sans serifs of the 1930s which had large x heights and round features intended to promote readability on signs.

- *download* - Trebuchet MS for Windows 9x, NT and Windows 2000
  locations - current server | Redmond | Tokyo | London
  file details - trebuc32.exe - 348KB self installing file
  font details - version 1.22 (i) - WGL4 character set

- *download* - Trebuchet MS for Windows 3.1 and 3.11
  locations - current server | Redmond | Tokyo | London
  file details - trebuc.exe - 174KB self extracting archive
  font details - version 1.00 (i)

- *download* - Trebuchet MS for Apple Mac OS
  locations - current server | Redmond | Tokyo | London
  file details - Trebuchet.sit.hqx - 315KB BinHex
  font details - version 1.15

Georgia, **Georgia Bold**, *Georgia Italic*, ***Georgia Bold Italic***

Georgia by Matthew Carter, hinted by Thomas Rickner.

2

3

Here is some text in one of the Microsoft web standard display fonts in this case Arial Black

Here is some text in one of the Microsoft web standard display fonts in this case Impact

Here is some text in one of the Microsoft web standard display fonts in this case Comic Sans

1 *Try out your webpages in each of the main body copy fonts to see which works best for you. Georgia and Verdana both have larger x-heights, which make them better for smaller sizes, but I find Arial and Times New Roman easier reading for longer stretches.*

2 *Microsoft's general software dominance makes it the main source of Web fonts. The core fonts are likely to be installed on most users' systems and are also available for free download from the Microsoft typography Web site:* **www.microsoft.com/ typography.**

3 *For display type, Microsoft provides a further range of standard faces that are designed to have more impact and can create a very different feel on a page.*

4 *Remember to specify your type with a font list, or it might end up being displayed in the browser's default of Times.*

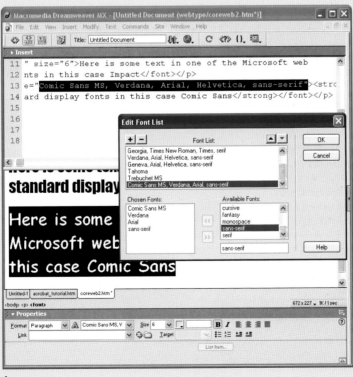

4

¹¹⁶ FONT-EMBEDDING TECHNOLOGIES

By specifying common font standards in font lists, we can begin to add some typographical variety to our pages. But it's still a long way away from the typographic freedom of print. What we really need is some way to make any font available via the Web. That's exactly what is promised by a technology called font embedding. Font-embedding packages up the scalable font outline itself into a file format that a browser can read and display whenever the HTML code references it.

The first major font-embedding technology, called TrueDoc, was developed by the Bitstream font foundry and championed by Netscape. To make use of it today, you can simply add a link to one of a range of "dynamic fonts" provided on the *www.truedoc.com* site. With just a few lines of code you can start using a whole host of completely new faces that can really make your pages stand out.

TrueDoc proved that font embedding works, but it has a number of drawbacks. The range of presupplied dynamic fonts is limited; the PFR file sizes tend to be large and slow to download; and, without hinting, the quality of body text can be poor. Even worse, what used to be TrueDoc's biggest strength, its cross-platform browser support, has become its major weakness. Users of the most common browser, Internet Explorer, are asked to install a plug-in player before they can access your site. Even worse, the latest Netscape browser has dropped its support for PFRs completely.

It might look like the idea of font embedding is finished before it's even begun—but don't despair. The potential of delivering any font over the Web is too good to give up on, and another candidate has stepped in to take up the challenge. What's more, none of the limitations that prevented TrueDoc from taking off apply to this new technology. It's a font-embedding system that works with just about any typeface, keeps font file sizes to a minimum, produces high-quality hinted results, and works natively with Internet Explorer. It's also free and it comes from Microsoft! WEFT (Web Embedding Fonts Tool) must be the Web's best-kept secret.

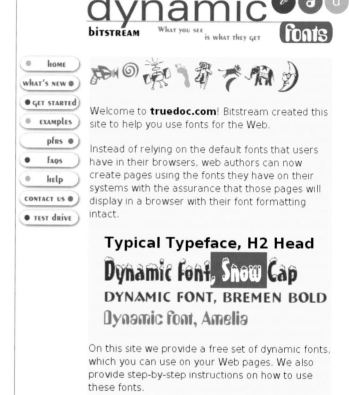

1

2

```
<HTML>
<HEAD>
<TITLE>My Resume</TITLE>

<LINK REL="FONTDEF" SRC="http://www.truedoc.com/pfrs/AmeriGarmnd.pfr">
<LINK REL="FONTDEF" SRC="http://www.truedoc.com/pfrs/BakerSignet.pfr">

<SCRIPT LANGUAGE="JavaScript" SRC="http://www.truedoc.com/activex/tdserver.js">
</SCRIPT>
<link>

<STYLE TYPE="text/css">
P {
    font-family: "AmeriG
    size: 3;
    color: #000000;
}
</STYLE>
</HEAD>

<BODY>

<FONT FACE="BakerSigne
```

3

1 *The TrueDoc site, at* **www.truedoc.com,** *is devoted to Bitstream's TrueDoc font embedding technology.*

2 *There are a range of dynamic fonts on the site, which you can explore and link to for your own projects.*

3 *To start using the TrueDoc fonts, all you need to do is to add a couple of lines of code to your HTML files.*

4 *The major modern font-embedding technology comes from Microsoft in the form of the free WEFT utility. Visit* **http://www.microsoft.com/typo graphy/web/embedding/weft3/** *to download it.*

5|6 *Using WEFT, you can create webpages that are viewable by any Internet Explorer user, and still use any of your installed fonts.*

All Products | Support | Search | Microsoft.com Guide

Microsoft

Microsoft Typography | ...on the Web | ...embedding | Microsoft WEFT 3

Microsoft WEFT 3

About WEFT

The Web Embedding Fonts Tool 'WEFT', lets Web authors create 'font objects' that are linked to their Web pages so that when an Internet Explorer user views the pages they'll see them displayed in the font style contained within the font object.

WEFT users Web community

The Microsoft WEFT users Web Community is an open community with over one thousand members. Anyone can join and contribute questions, answers, tips and tricks. If you've been using WEFT for a while or are new to the tool be sure

news

Release notes

- WEFT 3 overview
- Download page
- Database generation
- Available fonts
- WEFT 3 wizard
  - Set user information
  - Add Web pages
  - Analyzing Web pages
  - Fonts to embed
  - Create font objects
  - Publishing Web pages
  - Finished
- Troubleshooting and testing
- WEFT 3 tutorial

4

5

RECIPES FOR HEALTHIER EATING

Oven Baked or Stove Top Courgettes

Follow this quick and easy recipe for a delicious side dish or main entree. Courgettes are available nearly all year round and make a healthy and nutritious meal.

Slice the courgettes lengthwise and remove the seeds and pith. Sprinkle some salt over the shells and let sit for a few minutes, then fill the hollow with diced vegetables, mixed rice or minced beef and place in oven at 375F for 25 minutes. Top with grated cheese. Alternatively, if you are strapped for time try this quick and easy recipe.

6

118 **PROJECT 16:**

FONT-EMBEDDING WITH WEFT

So let's see how Microsoft's font-embedding system works in practice. Could this really be the Holy Grail of typographic tools for the hard-pressed Web designer? Let's see...

❶ First of all, create a sample page with a heading, a sub-heading, and some body copy. By default the type will appear as Times New Roman, but using the <font face="..."> tag with a typical font list—Arial, Helvetica, sans-serif—we can force all the copy to a more modern sans-serif typeface.

❷ Now let's open WEFT and see just what fonts are available to us. Using the *View>Available Fonts* command, you can see all of your currently installed fonts. Fonts that cannot be embedded are marked with a red cross. AvantGarde will work.

❸ Now we can return to our page and edit the <font> tags to add in "AvantGarde Bk BT" before Arial in each of our font lists (make sure you get the spelling and case exactly right). Because the font is installed locally on our system, it appears in Dreamweaver's layout window and the change is certainly dramatic. Suddenly our type comes to life with lots more character. It certainly works well for our heading and sub-heading, but, predictably, it's a step backward in terms of readability for the body copy. There just aren't enough pixels to do the typeface justice. Let's keep headings in AvantGarde, but set the body copy in Arial.

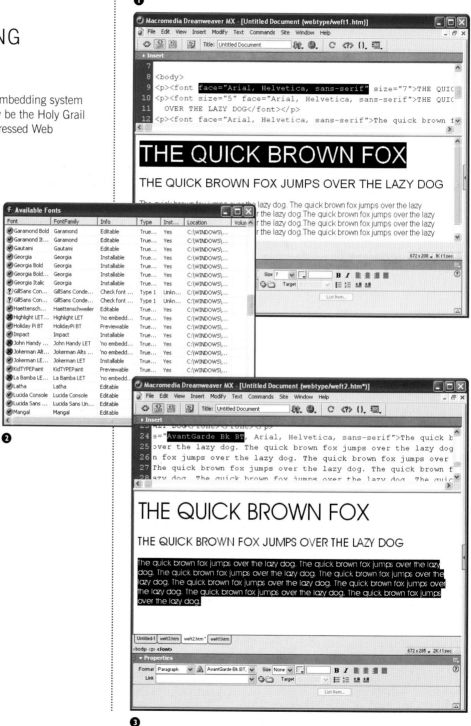

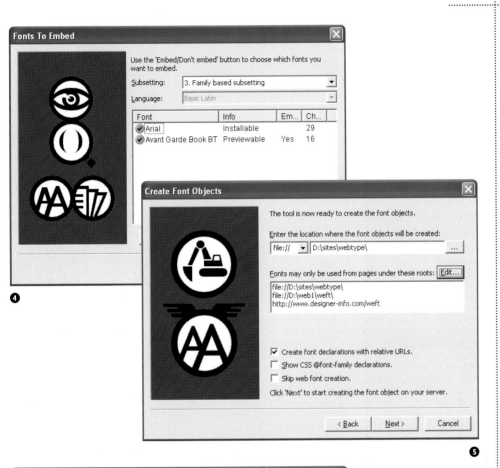

4 If we posted our page to the Web like this, the vast majority of end users wouldn't have AvantGarde on their systems, so the type would default back to Arial/Helvetica. That's where the WEFT wizard comes in. Firstly, we have to tell it which file to process; WEFT will then look for all font references and present the *Fonts to Embed* dialog. We can cut down on the final file size by setting Arial not to embed, as we can assume that the end user will have either this or Helvetica installed.

5 Next, in the *Create Font Objects* dialog, we have to set the location where the files will be created. You also have to set the locations from which the font will be accessed—in particular, the address of your website (if you didn't lock the font object to a particular site like this, then anyone could link to your font).

6 Click on *OK* and WEFT creates the Embedded OpenType EOT font object file (in this case, 7k in size) and also automatically updates the page's HTML code to link to it. Once both the page and EOT file are posted to the site that you specified earlier, any Internet Explorer users will be able to see the page just as it appears on your local system with the AvantGarde font in place. Netscape users aren't so lucky, but, thanks to the use of the font list, they'll still be able to see the page in Arial or Helvetica, so they aren't any worse off than they were before.

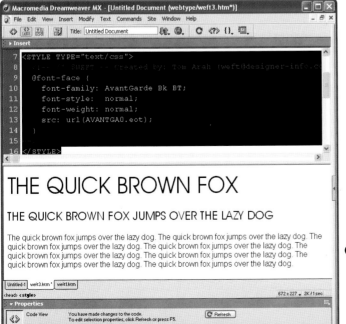

120 SOURCING WEB FONTS

The ability to specify and actually embed any font makes a huge difference. For body copy, it usually doesn't make sense to use an unusual face because it won't be fully optimized for onscreen reading at low resolution. But for headings, and wherever we want to add some typographic impact, we can now add any font that catches our eye. The world is our oyster, typographically speaking—so what's the best source of fonts?

The first thing to check is whether you might already have the perfect font ready to go. These days, all operating systems come with a wide selection of body and display fonts. And each time you add a new application, there's a strong chance that it will add some extra fonts of its own.

2

1

3

4

You might also have a wider choice than you realize. Many design-oriented applications come with a range of extra fonts that are installed only if you specifically ask for them to be. Perhaps the best value collection is the range of over 1,000 fonts that come with CorelDraw.

The best source for the widest range of fonts is the Web. All the major type foundries have made their collections available online, and a number of sites, such as *www.fontpool.com* and *www.fonts.com*, are dedicated to helping you find the font you need.

Best of all, you might well be able to find the font you need for free. The number of free fonts available on the Web is enormous and growing rapidly. While they might not be of the highest quality or have a complete character set (check for currency symbols), this usually makes a difference only for body copy destined for print. For onscreen use as high-impact display type, their quality is more than good enough. Simply enter "free fonts" into any search engine and you can begin finding the perfect typeface that, once embedded, will really make your site stand out.

1 *Take a look in your font directory and you're likely to find hundreds of fonts already installed. Many applications come with their own set of fonts that are automatically installed.*

2 *CorelDraw comes with over 1000 fonts and its own dedicated Font Navigator utility so that you can see what a typeface looks like before installing it.*

3|4 *The Web itself acts as the perfect distribution medium for fonts. Adobe offers thousands of fonts, including collections specially optimized for Web use.*

5 *Enter "free fonts" into your favorite search engine and you'll be bombarded with options.*

6 *My current favorite source of hundreds of high-quality free fonts is www.autofx.com.*

5

6

122 PROJECT 17:

EMBEDDED FONT SHOWCASE

So let's put font-embedding to work on a real project. Imagine our heavy metal band Trancystor has taken off and gone global, and that we're now producing a fan site dedicated to celebrating their back catalogue. Welcome to The Cysterhood!

❶ First of all, it's important to recognize that font-embedding can only go so far. For our sample page's body type, we're going to stick with a safe, screen-optimized, serif-based font list. For the band's name too, we don't have any of the control over distortion and styling effects that we do in a bitmap editor, so we're best sticking to our existing GIF logo.

❷ That still leaves plenty of scope for some typographical creativity. In particular, let's set up the page title to be written in the same Parry Hotter font that we downloaded from the Web. And let's set up the album title to use the second, rather more legible, font that we used for the logo's strapline. In both cases, the best way to specify the font is to set it up as the first choice in a <font> list. That way, we can quickly apply the fonts to our headings from the *Properties* panel.

❸ We can now add the same fonts to the rest of the site. When all the pages are ready, run WEFT. By pointing the program at our home page and setting WEFT to analyse all linked pages, you can process the entire site to produce master font files that all the pages are linked to, rather than separate files for each page.

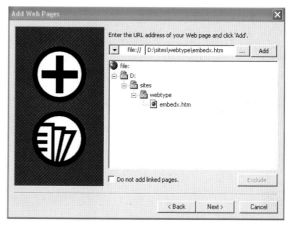

❹ The other major setting to make is to control the embedding process. Again, we can switch off all embedding of the body copy's Georgia font since this, or a reasonably close serif equivalent, should be available on most systems. Because the fonts we *do* want to embed are very graphical, we can specify just those characters we want to include, to ensure that we've cut our font object file sizes to the absolute minimum. The end result for this page are two files totaling just 17k—even better, these will be cached by the browser so that other pages will be able to use the same font objects without further downloading.

❺ And here's the end result seen in the latest Navigator. At first sight, it looks a major disappointment, but of course this is what we have to expect because EOT font files are supported in Internet Explorer only (currently at least). The good news is that Navigator users are no worse off than they would have been if we hadn't embedded the fonts. Navigator simply selects the next font on the font list.

❻ For Internet Explorer users, though, our Cysterhood site really stands out. Thanks to WEFT, it's an eye-catching individual in a world of Times and Helvetica-only clones.

escape
Escape

Text Size

Encoding

Source

Privacy Report

Full Screen

CSS Style definition

Category
Type
Background
Block
Box
Border
List
Positioning
Extensions

CSS Style definition for li

Category   List

Type
Background   Type: square
Block
Box   disc
Border
List   Bullet Image
Positioning
Extensions   Position

CSS Style definition for a

Category   Type
Type
Background
Block   Font: Trebuchet, Arial, Helvetica, sans-serif
Box
Border   Size: ____ pixels   Weight: bold
List
Positioning   Style: ____   Variant: ____
Extensions
                        Line Height: ____ pixels   Case: ____

                        Decoration: ☐ underline   Color: ☐ ____
                                    ☐ overline
                                    ☐ line-through
                                    ☐ blink
                                    ☑ none

                        OK   Cancel   Apply

Text

Indent   Ctrl+Alt+]

Outdent   Ctrl+Alt+[

Paragraph Format   ▸

Align   ▸

List   ▸

Font   ▸

Style   ▸

HTML Styles   ▸

CSS Styles   ▸   ✓ None
                              OK   Cancel   Apply

Size   ▸

Size Change   ▸   New CSS Style...

Color...   Edit Style Sheet...

                                 Attach Style Sheet...

Check Spelling Shift+F7   Export CSS Styles...

                                 Design Time Style Sheets

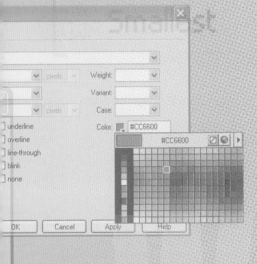

Cascading Style Sheets (CSS)

Everything would be so much simpler if we could just start again with a Web language dedicated to controlling the appearance of our webpages in the same way that HTML was designed to describe the page's content. In fact, this language does exist, is supported by all the latest browsers and authoring applications, and is set to revolutionize Web typography. So let's see what it is and how it works…

Ctrl+Shift+E

INTRODUCING HTML 4/CSS

Using the HTML 3.2 features that we looked at before, such as the various <table> and <font> tags, designers manage to exert some sort of layout and type control and have created the Web as we know it today. However, the limitations are still serious: font handling is restricted, there's virtually no control over type size, and absolutely no control over essential features such as word, line, and paragraph spacing.

Even worse, many of HTML 3.2's apparent solutions create their own problems. In particular, if you take a look at the HTML necessary to produce a typical webpage, you'll find that there's actually more code spent on the <table> and <font> tags than there is on the content! This not only makes editing the code far more difficult than it should be, it also means that the pages are slower to download and slower for the browser to interpret—the two cardinal sins of Web design.

HTML 3.2 makes the most of a bad job, but it's best seen as a temporary fix and certainly not as a secure foundation for the future. Given the chance, we'd be far better off starting again from scratch with a dedicated and powerful Web formatting language. Having said that, though, there are already billions of HTML-based pages out there and this vast amount of information can't just be ignored. It looks like we're stuck: unable to move on or to go back to the drawing board.

Don't despair; there is a solution. The CSS (Cascading Style Sheets) language was developed by the World Wide Web Consortium, the body in charge of developing HTML and all other open standards for the Web. The beauty of CSS is that it manages to pull off the near-impossible—providing new typographic power while working hand-in-hand with the existing HTML framework. In fact, the two work so well together that the major advance in the World Wide Web Consortium's HTML 4.0 specification wasn't a slew of new HTML tags but rather a way of integrating HTML with CSS.

1

David Bowie Discography

Space Oddity

The Man who sold the World

Hunky Dory

The Rise and Fall of Ziggy Stardust

Aladdin Sane

Pinups

Diamond Dogs

Young Americans

Station to Station

Hunky Dory

SIDE 1:

1. *Changes*
2. *Oh! You Pretty Things*
3. *Eight Line Poem*
4. *Life on Mars?*
5. *Kooks*
6. *Quicksand*

SIDE 2:

1. *Fill Your Heart*
2. *Andy Warhol*
3. *Song for Bob Dylan*
4. *Queen Bitch*
5. *The Bewlay Brothers*

Personnel: David Bowie (vocals, sax, guitar), Mick Ronson (guitar), Rick Wakeman (piano), Trevor Bolder (bass), Woody Woodmansey (drums)

Producer: Ken Scott

1971 was a turning-point for David Bowie. inatil ubliuremur. effre tea in vit, ut oporest dem rei pracci publi, in vens mere nostraven vena, con tereo, castatiam Mick Ronson te, Ti. An senius. Quium ia? Nos octorunum interrae num veret diena, que ina, intem ortium, quam, ad din dit.

Habes corum patrati temque tus, qua depero, et L. Serum de conte ducerenatus Mulicatum horeis conotilici publin tum re, nihilibus Tony Visconti publis aurnius hostraet L. Quita L. Simus, nos caectus viverit villissena, cupici sperissoltus cae incum ublintem et omnicis, estri porem, no. Fula omne elum dienicae inunterica; num hos, quit.

2

```
            <td colspan="3"><h3 align="right"><font face="Verdana, Arial, Helvetica, sans-serif">David
            Bowie Discography</font></h3></td>
        </tr>
        <tr>
            <td width="102" rowspan="4" valign="top"> <p><font size="-1"><strong><a href="spaceoddity.htm
            Oddity</font></a></strong></font></p>
            <p><font face="Verdana, Arial, Helvetica, sans-serif"><strong><font size="-1"><a href="them
            Man who sold the World</a></font></strong></font></p>
            <p><font face="Verdana, Arial, Helvetica, sans-serif"><strong><font size="-1"><a href="hunk
            Dory</a></font></strong></font></p>
            <p><font face="Verdana, Arial, Helvetica, sans-serif"><strong><font size="-1"><a href="link
            Rise and Fall of Ziggy Stardust</a></font></strong></font></p>
            <p><font face="Verdana, Arial, Helvetica, sans-serif"><strong><font size="-1"><b><a href="l
            Sane</a></b></font></strong></font></p>
            <p><b><strong><font size="-1" face="Verdana, Arial, Helvetica, sans-serif"><a href="link.ht
            <p><b><strong><font size="-1" face="Verdana, Arial, Helvetica, sans-serif"><a href="link.ht
            Dogs</a></font></strong></b></p>
            <p><b><strong><font size="-1" face="Verdana, Arial, Helvetica, sans-serif"><a href="link.ht
            Americans</a></font></strong></b></p>
            <p><b><strong><font size="-1" face="Verdana, Arial, Helvetica, sans-serif"><a href="link.ht
            to Station</a></font></strong></b></p></td>
            <td height="76" colspan="2" valign="top" bgcolor="#FF9900"><font size="7" face="Georgia, Time
            Dory</em></font></td>
        </tr>
        <tr>
            <td width="200" valign="top" bgcolor="#FFCC00"> <p><font face="Verdana, Arial, Helvetica, san
            1: </font></strong></font></p>
            <ol>
```

W3C WORLD WIDE WEB consortium.

Leading the Web to its Full Potential...

Activities | Technical Reports | Site Index | New Visitors | About W3C | Contact Us

The World Wide Web Consortium (W3C) develops interoperable technologies (specifications, guidelines, software, and tools) to lead the Web to its full potential. W3C is a forum for information, commerce, communication, and collective understanding. On this page, you'll find W3C news, links to W3C technologies and ways to get involved. New visitors can find help in *Finding Your Way at W3C*. We encourage you to learn more about W3C.

W3C A to Z

- Accessibility
- Amaya
- Annotea
- CC/PP
- CSS
- CSS Validator
- Device Independence
- DOM
- HTML
- HTML Tidy
- HTML Validator
- HTTP

► **XHTML 1.0 Second Edition Is a W3C Recommendation**

Google

3

W3C®

HTML 4.01 Specification

W3C Recommendation 24 December 1999

This version:
http://www.w3.org/TR/1999/REC-html401-19991224
(plain text [794Kb], gzip'ed tar archive of HTML files [371Kb], a zip archive of HTML files [405Kb], gzip'ed Postscript file [746Kb, 389 pages], gzip'ed PDF file [963Kb])
Latest version of HTML 4.01:
http://www.w3.org/TR/html401
Latest version of HTML 4:
http://www.w3.org/TR/html4
Latest version of HTML:
http://www.w3.org/TR/html

4

Learning CSS

Specs

CSS Validator

What's new?

W3C
Activities
Tech. reports
Translations
Software
Site index
Search
Nearby:
Style

CSS Browsers

CSS Test Suites

Authoring Tools

W3C Core Styles

Also: SAC, CSS3 roadmap, translations and up to Style

Cascading Style Sheets (CSS) is a simple mechanism for adding style (e.g. fonts, colors, spacing) to Web documents. Tutorials, books, mailing lists for users, etc. can be found on the "learning CSS" page. For background information on style sheets, see the Web style sheets page. Discussions about CSS are carried out on the (archived) www-style@w3.org mailing list and on comp.infosystems.www.authoring.stylesheets.

5

1 *HTML 3.2 has enabled us to take Web type design further than the developers of HTML ever envisaged.*

2 *Take a look at the underlying code, however, and you'll find that far more code is spent on formatting than on content!*

3 *The www.w3.org site is the home of the World Wide Web Consortium, which is in charge of the development of HTML and other open Web standards.*

4│5 *The latest version of HTML is HTML 4. What makes HTML 4 so radical is the way that it transfers type-formatting control to a completely new mark-up language—CSS (Cascading Style Sheets). Technical details of both can be found on the w3.org site. See* **http://www.w3.org/TR/html401**

128 **PROJECT 18:**

A FIRST CSS RULE

So how does CSS pull off this remarkable feat of working within the existing HTML framework while grafting on advanced new typographic power?

The answer lies in that original split between content and presentation that Tim Berners-Lee devised when he first invented HTML and its logical tag architecture. Because a tag doesn't actually specify anything about how the browser should display it, CSS can step in to fill the gap.

The easiest way to understand this is to see it in practice. We're going to jump ahead of ourselves slightly and create our first CSS rule. We'll see later how current Web-authoring applications help you control your CSS, but for the moment we'll take advantage of CSS's simple syntax to enter the code.

❶ First of all, let's set up a page with a number of repeat headings and some inline italicizing.

❷ Now let's switch to *Split* view and put the cursor in the <head> element just below the page title and type the following: <style>h1 {color:blue}</style>

It's worth thinking about what we are doing here. To begin with, it's clear from the right-angled brackets before and after that we are adding an HTML <style> tag. Within the tag, the "h1" clearly sets the scope that the CSS will affect, and is called the *Selector*. After it, within the curly brackets, comes the list of effects or *Declarations*. Each declaration takes the form of the Property (in this case color), followed by a colon and space and then the Value (in this case "blue"). Multiple declarations are separated by semi-colons. Together the selector and declarations make a rule—and there we have all the fundamentals of CSS syntax.

❸ So what effect does the rule have? Now when you click back in the layout window, you'll see that both <h1> elements have turned blue. It might not seem that exciting until you think about it a little more. The huge breakthrough is that all of the <h1> tags on the page have been updated by our one rule—there's no need to locally format each tag. This ensures consistency, makes our code much easier to edit and update, keeps download size down, and enables the browser to display the page much more quickly.

❹ That's not bad for starters. But we can be even more efficient by grouping selectors. First we need to copy the existing rule and change the h1 selector to "h2, h3, p" and change the color property value to "green." When we click back in the design window, all the rest of our text is automatically updated. It's also worth noting that our italicized text is also colored because it has "inherited" the current element's CSS formatting. Formatting our page like this with HTML 3.2 would have involved applying multiple <font> tags.

130 CSS BROWSER SUPPORT

We're beginning to see the advantages of CSS in terms of efficiency and speed, but let's not get carried away. As we know from HTML, unless a given capability unless is supported consistently by the main browsers, it usually ends up being more trouble than it's worth.

Sadly, this was certainly the case in the early days of CSS. The big problem wasn't that the browsers didn't support CSS—in fact, this isn't a problem at all for CSS, but rather a strength. CSS was grafted onto the existing HTML tag framework, if the browser doesn't know how to deal with a CSS rule, it simply ignores it. So that in our example, the headings would still appear as normal; they just wouldn't be colored. In other words, CSS can "degrade gracefully."

The real problem comes from browsers that claim to support CSS but only half-implement a feature. The end result is that they try and interpret the rule, but end up turning your layout into a dog's dinner. Worse is the fact that you can't implement CSS for those users whose browsers do behave, because of those users whose browsers don't!

For a while, it looked like patchy browser support was going to kill CSS before it was even born. Thankfully, the Web is a fast changing world. These days CSS is a mature technology—it was first released in 1996!—and most modern browsers claim to support the core CSS features.

Having said this, it's still a good idea always to check your pages against the two major browsers, Internet Explorer and Netscape Navigator, and any other browsers or browser version that you know your site visitors regularly use. It's also sensible to play safe. We'll look at the updated CSS2 specifications later (see page 174) but until browser support is more robust it's wise to stick to CSS1. Don't worry—it still offers plenty of type-based power.

The CSShark Answers FAQs
The CSS Know-How Site

CSS and Netscape 4.xx Issues

Home
CSS FAQs
Basics
NN4 Issues
  2 Sheets
  Background
  Fonts
  Table, List
  Forms
  Margins
  Mixed Bag
Tutorial
Links
Books

Hosted by
chicagowebs

The market share of browsers that do not support any CSS is now below 0.5%. Therefore web developers have more freedom to actually separate content (HTML) and presentation (CSS).

The biggest challenges that web developers face when implementing CSS is backwards compatibility and browser support.

The problem is that most browser have been developed at a time when CSS was still in 'draft-mode' and by no means a web standard. Some browsers have been constantly updated since then, others not. Blooberry has a fascinating timeline for browsers and the history of CSS.

Today we have > 80% IE 5.0, 5.5 and IE6, less than 10% NN4.xx and approximately 3.5% IE4. Netscape 6, Opera and other browsers are fighting for the rest (http://www.upsdell.com/BrowserNews/stat.htm).

In short, sweet words: CSS1 support is at least partially available for more than 96% of the current browser population, with a good CSS2 support for about 80% of today's browsers.

In terms of backwards compatibility these numbers mean: we have some support for CSS since versions 4 – NN and IE. Unfortunately, NN 4.xx had only minor and cosmetic updates while Explorer was able to incorporate more CSS features, and re-work buggy implementations.

With the total rehash of Netscape 6 and Explorer 6 already released we can confidently look into the future, but in the meantime we have to live with a certain percentage of Netscape 4 browsers.

The issues that surface quite often in Newsgroups are:

- Why use different styles for NN and IE - and how?
- Background
- Font: Sizes and Inheritance
- Tables, Lists
- Forms

Basic Concepts

Property or Value		Windows95/98/NT									Macintosh					
		Nav4	Nav6	IE3	IE4	IE5	IE55	Op3	Op4	Op5	Nav4	Nav6	IE3	IE4	IE5	
1.1	Containment in HTML	P	Y	P	Q	Q	Q	Y	Y	Y	P	Y	B	Y	Y	
	LINK	Y	Y	Y	Y	Y	Y	Y	Y	Y	Y	Y	B	Y	Y	
	\<STYLE>...\</STYLE>	Y	Y	Y	Y	Y	Y	Y	Y	Y	Y	Y	Y	Y	Y	
	@import	N	Y	N	Q	Q	Q	Y	Y	Y	N	Y	N	Y	Y	[note]
	\<x STYLE="dec;">	B	Y	Y	Y	Y	Y	Y	Y	Y	B	Y	Y	Y	Y	[note]
1.2	Grouping	Y	Y	N	Y	Y	Y	Y	Y	Y	Y	Y	Y	Y	Y	
	x, y, z (dec;)	Y	Y	N	Y	Y	Y	Y	Y	Y	Y	Y	Y	Y	Y	
1.3	Inheritance	B	Y	P	Y	Y	Y	Y	Y	Y	B	Y	B	Y	Y	[note]
	(inherited values)	B	Y	P	Y	Y	Y	Y	Y	Y	B	Y	B	Y	Y	
1.4	Class selector	Y	Y	B	Q	Q	Q	Y	Y	Y	Y	Y	B	Y	Y	[note]
	.class	Y	Y	B	Q	Q	Q	Y	Y	Y	Y	Y	B	Y	Y	
1.5	ID selector	B	Y	B	B	B	B	Y	Y	Y	B	Y	B	B	Y	[note]
	#ID	B	Y	B	B	B	B	Y	Y	Y	B	Y	B	B	Y	
1.6	Contextual selectors	Y	Y	Y	Y	Y	Y	Y	Y	Y	B	Y	P	Y	Y	
	x y z (dec;)	Y	Y	Y	Y	Y	Y	Y	Y	Y	B	Y	P	Y	Y	[note]
1.7	Comments	Y	Y	B	Y	Y	Y	Y	Y	Y	Y	Y	Y	Y	Y	
	/* comment */	Y	Y	B	Y	Y	Y	Y	Y	Y	Y	Y	Y	Y	Y	

Pseudo-Classes and Pseudo-Elements

Property or Value		Windows95/98/NT									Macintosh					
		Nav4	Nav6	IE3	IE4	IE5	IE55	Op3	Op4	Op5	Nav4	Nav6	IE3	IE4	IE5	
2.1	anchor	P	Y	N	Y	Y	Y	P	P	Y	P	Y	B	Y	Y	
	:link	Y	Y	N	Y	Y	Y	Y	Y	Y	Y	Y	B	Y	Y	
	:active	N	Y	N	Y	Y	Y	N	N	Y	N	Y	N	Y	Y	
	:visited	N	Y	N	Y	Y	Y	Y	Y	Y	N	Y	N	Y	Y	
2.3	first-line	N	Y	N	N	Y	Y	Y	Y	Y	N	Y	B	N	Y	[note]
	:first-line	N	Y	N	N	Y	Y	Y	Y	Y	N	Y	B	N	Y	
2.4	first-letter	N	Y	N	N	Y	Y	Y	Y	Y	N	Y	B	N	Y	[note]
	:first-letter	N	Y	N	N	Y	Y	Y	Y	Y	N	Y	B	N	Y	

1

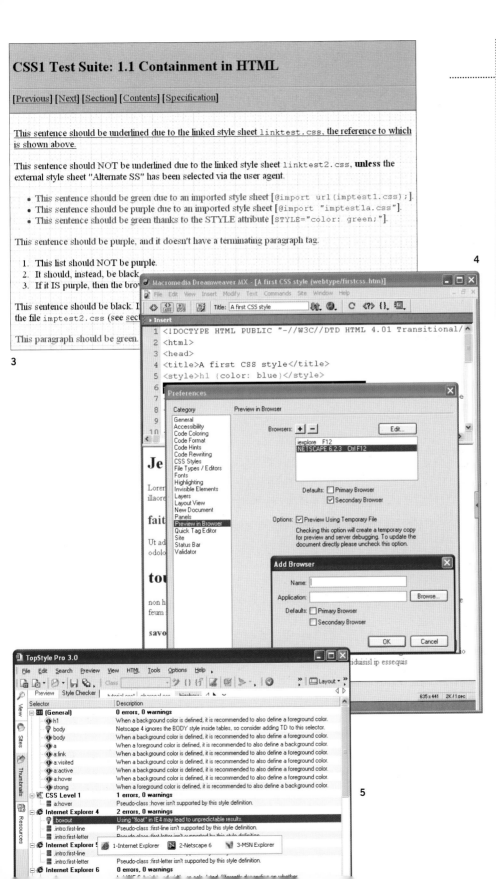

CSS1 Test Suite: 1.1 Containment in HTML

[Previous] [Next] [Section] [Contents] [Specification]

This sentence should be underlined due to the linked style sheet linktest.css, the reference to which is shown above.

This sentence should NOT be underlined due to the linked style sheet linktest2.css, **unless the** external style sheet "Alternate SS" has been selected via the user agent.

- This sentence should be green due to an imported style sheet [@import url(imptest1.css);].
- This sentence should be purple due to an imported style sheet [@import "imptest1a.css"].
- This sentence should be green thanks to the STYLE attribute [STYLE="color: green;"].

This sentence should be purple, and it doesn't have a terminating paragraph tag.

1. This list should NOT be purple.
2. It should, instead, be black
3. If it IS purple, then the brow

This sentence should be black. I
the file imptest2.css (see sect

This paragraph should be green.

3

4

1 *The worst CSS offender was Netscape 4. To find out about issues and workarounds, visit* **www.mako4css.com/Issues .htm**. *Fortunately, there are relatively few users still using Netscape 4 and so the onus is on the user to upgrade rather than for the author to cater to the lowest common denominator.*

2 *Eric Meyer keeps a site listing giving full details of the main browsers' CSS support at* **www.webreview.com**. *Before basing your entire design around a particular CSS feature, it's always advisable to check to see if there are browsers which don't support it.*

3 *Thanks to improved testing, CSS browser support has improved dramatically.*

4 *You should still always preview your pages in the two main browsers, Internet Explorer and Netscape Navigator, and any other browsers that you know your site visitors use.*

5 *Using a program like TopStyle Pro, you can check your style sheets against the CSS capabilities of all the most common browsers.*

132 CSS APPLICATION SUPPORT

Now that browser support is in place, CSS has become fully established and all the major Web-authoring applications now provide comprehensive CSS capabilities and features.

Access to CSS styling in Microsoft FrontPage is made through the *Format>Style* dialog, which lets you change existing HTML tag formatting with the *Modify...* command or create your own with the *New...* command. The formatting options on offer are split into five main categories *Font, Paragraph, Border, Numbering,* and *Position*. The main thrust of FrontPage's CSS handling is to try and make it seem similar to the style formatting in a program like Word. Sadly, FrontPage suggests that designing for the Web is easier than it actually is and therefore isn't the best way to get the most out of your CSS.

CSS control in Adobe GoLive is much less user-friendly, but ultimately much more powerful. To begin using CSS in GoLive, you need to open the dedicated *CSS Editor*. Here you are thrown right in the deep end with the need to understand CSS concepts such as elements, classes, and IDs before you can begin formatting your styles with the *Inspector* palette. It's a steep learning curve, but once you've mastered it, GoLive offers state-of-the-art control with instant access to all CSS styling, including direct code-editing.

A good middle ground is provided by Macromedia Dreamweaver. This makes it easy to begin using CSS with the *CSS Styles* panel's *New CSS Style* command for creating your styles. You also have plenty of advanced help on hand with the *Style Definition* dialog and the *CSS Reference*.

If you want absolute top-of-the-range power, there are even dedicated CSS authoring tools such as TopStyle Pro, which offer unique features such as the ability to validate your style sheets against multiple browsers.

Ultimately, though, it's important to recognize that CSS, just like HTML, is built on its code. If you know what you are doing, you can create and control your CSS formatting equally well in any authoring package—and, in fact, in any text editor.

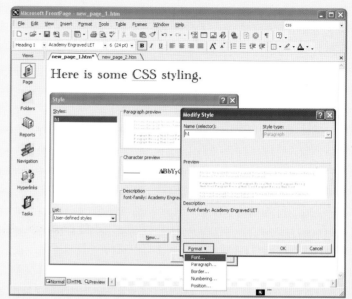

1

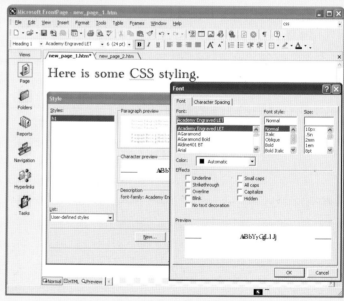

2

1 A CSS style is treated very much like a word processor style in FrontPage.

2 Sadly, FrontPage isn't a reliable middleman. For example, FrontPage's way of applying a font through CSS certainly makes life simple, but you really need to do it via a font list to cater for users without the font installed.

3 GoLive's CSS capabilities are harder to get to grips with, but offer much more reliable control.

4 With features such as its CSS Styles panel and full CSS Reference, Dreamweaver offers good usability and power.

5 TopStyle Pro from Bradbury Software offers dedicated standalone CSS editing.

6 Because CSS is code-based, you can actually take complete control of your Web type's formatting in even the simplest and most basic text editor.

3

4

5

6

134

PROJECT 19:
CSS TYPE BASICS

We've seen that CSS is another mark-up language very much like HTML and that it can be integrated into the HTML page. Now we're going to explore what it can do. In particular, we're going to see how CSS deals with the core typographic features that we've seen HTML handle.

❶ First of all, let's create a page with a couple of <h1> heading tags and a few <p> body paragraphs. Now, using Dreamweaver's *CSS Styles* palette's *New CSS Style* command, let's decide to *Redefine* the <p> tag for *This Document Only*.

❷ After the restrictions of HTML, the range of options in the *CSS Style Definition* dialog seems quite intimidating, with no less than eight different categories to explore, from *Type* through to *Extensions*. We're not going to run before we can walk, so let's look at the first and most important *Type* category. Using the *Font* drop-down, you have access to exactly the same font lists we're used to, so let's set this to "Arial, Helvetica, sans-serif." To preview the effect of your settings, you can click on *Apply* and, when you're happy with it, click on *OK*. Thanks to CSS, you'll see that your single setting automatically changes the appearance of all your <p> paragraphs—it's that simple.

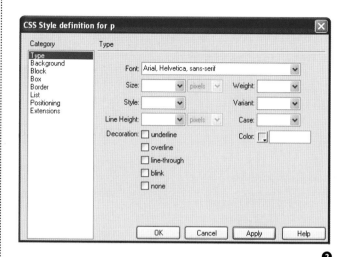

❷

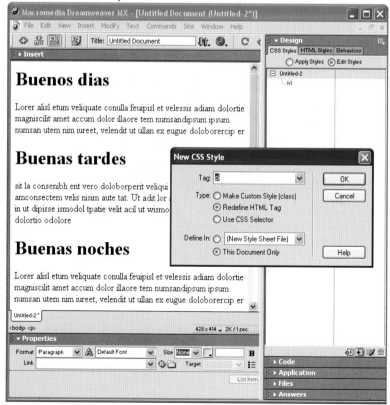

❶

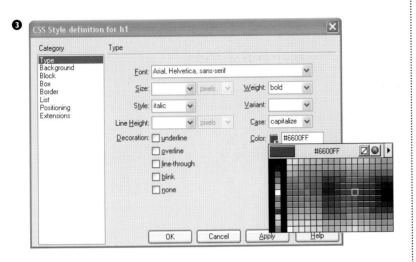

❸ Now let's go through the same procedure, this time redefining our <h1> tags. Again let's set the *Font* drop-down so that our headings share the same sans serif font list. And this time, let's explore Dreamweaver's *CSS Style Definition* dialog's *Type* category a bit more. We're going to come back to some of the settings shortly, but can set the *Style* to *Italic* and the *Weight* to *Bold*. Notice that CSS lets you specify weight in up to nine levels from 100 to 900—which could be useful in the future with typefaces that can be varied on the fly. We can also break some new ground by setting the *Case* parameter to *Capitalized*, which forces the first letter of every word in our headings to be set in uppercase and everything else in lowercase. This is a good feature for ensuring consistently formatted headings. Finally, with the *Color* drop-down, you can quickly specify any of the Web-safe colors. Dreamweaver automatically converts your choice to the necessary hexadecimal code.

❹ Take a look at the CSS code that Dreamweaver has added for us. As you'd expect, it takes the same form as the embedded rule that we created earlier with a <style> tag, containing selectors and declarations. The major difference is that to make it easier to understand, Dreamweaver automatically splits up the declarations onto their own lines.

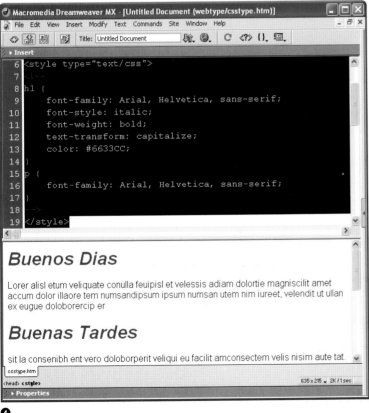

136 PROJECT 20:
CSS TYPE SIZE

Now we're ready to see how CSS addresses the long-standing problem of handling type size with its {font-size} property.

First of all, as you'd expect, you can mimic HTML's seven in-built sizes. For some reason, these aren't numbered but instead given names ranging from "xx-small" to "xx-large." As we've seen, the problem is that there is no consistency to the way browsers interpret these measures—though at least you know that "medium" will always be bigger than "small."

Where CSS begins to show its strength is in its relative size handling. Just like HTML's <small> and <big> tags, you can move up or down the 7-stage scale with the {font-size} property's "smaller" and "larger" values. Even more control is offered with the ability to set "percentages" and "ems." By setting {font-size} to "200%" or "2 em" for an inline tag such as <strong>, the type will be exactly twice its parent element's size. "Em" refers to the width of a letter "m" in each typeface. In this case, "1em" means 100% of the default font size.

With CSS, you can at last specify that your heading should be 36 points, or whichever size your prefer. Not only that, but CSS also provides an even better measure: pixels. If you set your heading style's {font-size} property to "48 px," you can be sure that that's exactly how big it will be—on both PC and Mac!

But don't get carried away. As ever, it comes down to a question of browser support. To begin with, some older browsers interpret pixels literally when it comes to print. This means that, if the end user prints your webpage, the type will be unreadably small. The bigger downside is that all browsers currently treat absolute measures as absolutely fixed, so the end user can't increase their body size.

Eventually browsers will catch up and, when they do, setting your type size in pixels has to be the way forward. In the meantime, it's left to the individual designer to decide whether flexible accessibility or absolute control is best.

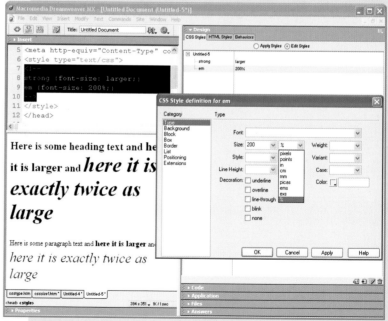

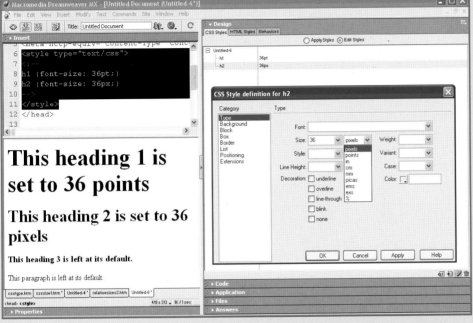

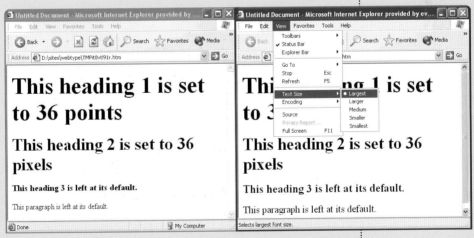

❹

❶ *CSS lets you specify HTML's built-in sizes by name—used here to make sure that <h1> is displayed at the largest "xx-large" size equivalent to <font size="7">.*

❷ *Using relative units, you can set sizes relative to the parent element. Here we've redefined the <strong> tag's {font-size} property to a value of "larger" and the <em> tag to "200%."*

❸ *The huge strength of CSS is the ability to set absolute sizes in points and pixels.*

❹ *The problem with absolute sizes is that current browsers don't let the end user override them. Notice how the bottom two paragraphs can change in size, but the top two are fixed.*

138 INSPIRATION:

THE W3C CORE STYLE SAMPLER

There is no need to be nervous about CSS, but if you don't quite feel ready to get to grips with the code, there is an easy way of seeing how using CSS could improve your work. Visit *www.w3.org/StyleSheets/Core/preview*—it's part of the World Wide Web Consortium's (W3C) site and is designed to show users how they can put CSS to use on their own projects.

1 *When you arrive at the W3C Core Style Sampler page, you are presented with a clean no-frills interface. There's no mass of background information, just the simple instruction, "To sample one of the W3C Core Styles, select a style sheet and a test document from the form below. "This is followed by a list of eight stylesheets and five sample documents. This page is actually itself formatted with the Swiss stylesheet and is an embodiment of the Google form of design—simple but efficient.*

2 *Make your selection, then click on the simple text-based Show me! button and your sample document quickly appears formatted according to the stylesheet you selected. Here I've selected the "Modernist" option, which provides a strong and slightly out-of-the-ordinary major heading based on the extra bold, condensed sans serif Impact (part of the Microsoft core web fonts); a contrasting sub-heading based on Arial bold; and body copy based on Arial at a large and eminently readable size. The type spacing is just as important as the choice of fonts, and a wide left margin and deep leading again ensures maximum readability.*

W3C Core Style Sampler

To sample one of the W3C Core Styles, select a style sheet and a test document from the form below:

Select a style sheet
○ "Oldstyle"
○ "Modernist"
○ "Midnight"
○ "Ultramarine"
○ "Swiss"
○ "Chocolate"
○ "Traditional"
◉ "Steely"
○ None/default (show the document selected below wit

Select a test document
◉ XML, Java, and the Future of the Web
○ Cascading Style Sheets (CSS) Level 1 Specification
○ Shame and War Revisited
○ HTML Element Sampler
○ Show me only the stylesheet I selected above.

[Show me!]

1

XML, Java, and the future of the Web

Jon Bosak, Sun Microsystems
Last revised 1997.03.10

Introduction

The extraordinary growth of the World Wide Web has been fueled by the ability it gives authors to easily and cheaply distribute electronic documents to an international audience. As Web documents have become larger and more complex, however, Web content providers have begun to experience the limitations of a medium that does not provide the extensibility, structure, and data checking needed for large-scale commercial publishing. The ability of Java applets to embed powerful data manipulation capabilities in Web clients makes even clearer the limitations of current methods for the transmittal of document data.

To address the requirements of commercial Web publishing and enable the further expansion of Web technology into new domains of distributed document processing, the World Wide Web Consortium has developed an Extensible Markup Language (XML) for applications that require functionality beyond the current Hypertext Markup Language (HTML). **This paper** [0] describes the XML effort and discusses new kinds of Java-based Web applications made possible by XML.

XML, Java, and the future of the Web

Jon Bosak, Sun Microsystems
Last revised 1997.03.10

Introduction

The extraordinary growth of the World Wide Web has been fueled by the ability it gives authors to easily and cheaply distribute electronic documents to an international audience. As Web documents have become larger and more complex, however, Web content providers have begun to experience the limitations of a medium that does not provide the extensibility, structure, and data checking needed for large-scale commercial publishing. The ability of Java applets to embed powerful data manipulation capabilities in Web clients makes even clearer the limitations of current methods for the transmittal of document data.

To address the requirements of commercial Web publishing and enable the further expansion of Web technology into new domains of distributed document processing, the World Wide Web Consortium has developed an Extensible Markup Language (XML) for applications that require functionality beyond the current Hypertext Markup Language (HTML). **This paper** [0] describes the XML effort and discusses new kinds of Java-based Web applications made possible by XML.

```
          <LINK REL="Copyright" HREF="http://css.nu/copyright.html">
<link rel=stylesheet href="http://www.w3.org/StyleSheets/Core/Midnight"
type="text/css"><META http-equiv="Content-Style-Type" content='text/css'>
<META NAME="keywords" content="Cascading Style Sheets, CSS, Bugs, Pointers, DHTML,
XSL, DSSSL, Snippets">
<LINK REV="made" HREF="mailto:sue@css.nu">
```

CSS Pointers

this document is located at...
<URI:**http://css.nu/pointers/index2.html**>

❖ CSS Pointers Menu ❖

These links were compiled by **Toby Brown**, **Jan Roland Eriksson**, and Sue Sims. Additional information about the authors' CSS philosophies and usage may be found **online**. Suggestions and criticisms are welcome.

New Items are flagged with the [new !] notagif. **(TM)** Links which have been moved to the archives are marked with {A}.

- CSS from the W3C
- CSS from Todd Fahrner
- XSL/XML/DSSSL
- Books and Reviews
- Bugs and Tests
- Implementation Solutions
- CSS Columns
- Browser Support
- Authoring Tools

3 *Select another stylesheet—in this case, "Midnight"—and the results for the same document are totally different. Rather than white, the background is a striking black: a fact highlighted by the wide margins, which produce a large generous area of solid black space. The body font here is smaller and, with less leading and less contrast between the cream text and black background, there's a danger that the text will be unreadable. However this is countered by the use of Verdana which, thanks to its large x-height, makes the absolute most of every pixel.*

4 *Alternatively, you can put any of these core styles to work for you immediately and with just one line of code! As another source for CSS information - the CSS Pointers Group site at* **http://css.nu/pointers/ index2.html** *- demonstrates, you are allowed and encouraged to link your own pages to the CSS styles on the W3C's site to format your own HTML elements.*

CSS is all about efficient Web type handling and the CSS Core Style Sampler site embodies this in action.

140 PROJECT 21:
CORE CSS SHOWCASE

We now understand the basics of CSS type-handling so let's see it in practice on a real world project. To highlight how HTML 4/CSS's type handling compares to HTML 3.2's, let's see how it copes with producing another discography project similar to the one we produced earlier. You'll notice straight-away from the look and feel of the project that there is something more sophisticated about it; it feels more "designed," although the differences are subtle to the untrained eye. But that's what good design's all about, isn't it?

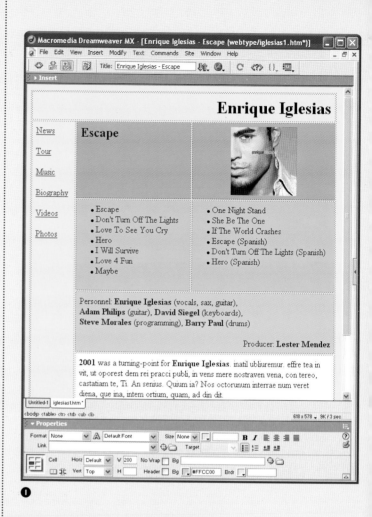

❶ To begin, give yourself a bit of a head-start by copying the table framework that we used last time, adding some new text and formatting this with some of the core HTML tags: <h1> for the page title; <h2> for the album title; <a> anchor tags for the links; <li> tags for the list items; <p> tags for the body text; and <strong> tags for the inline emboldening.

❷ Once this is in place, our first formatting task is to set all the type to sans serif. The easiest way to do this is to create a rule, setting the <body> tag's {font-face} property to the common "Verdana, Arial, Helvetica, sans-serif" font list. Unfortunately, not all browsers are great at handling this (it's a similar situation to HTML 3.2's <basefont> tag). So, to play it safe, remember to set the same font list for each of the CSS rules on the page as you create them.

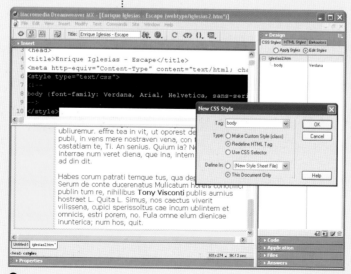

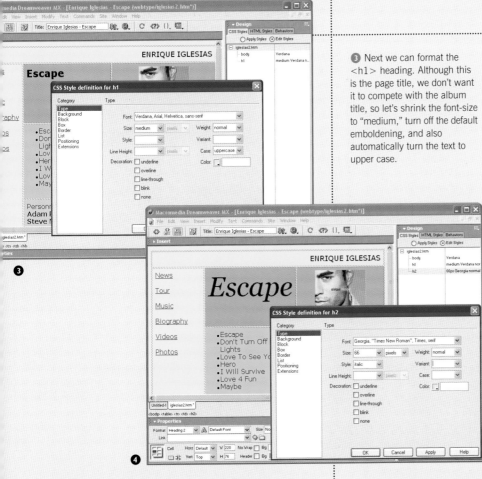

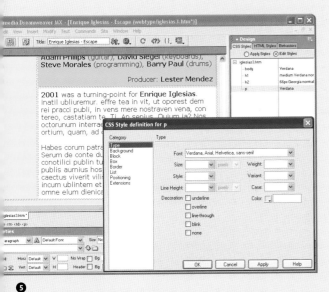

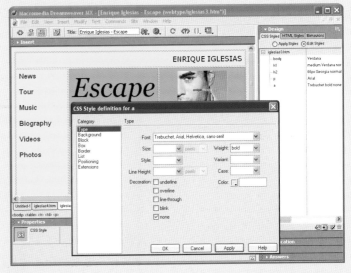

3 Next we can format the <h1> heading. Although this is the page title, we don't want it to compete with the album title, so let's shrink the font-size to "medium," turn off the default emboldening, and also automatically turn the text to upper case.

4 We want the <h2> album title to stand out, so change the typeface to an italicized serif—in this case, Georgia. In terms of size, we want the type to fill the column. Set the font size to exactly 66 pixels. This will appear identically on both Mac and PC platforms.

5 It's also tempting to set the body text <p> tags to a pixel-based size for cross-platform consistency, but that wouldn't suit all viewers, especially those with limited vision. Use defaults.

6 Now we can format the list of links down the left-hand column by setting a CSS style for the <a> tag. The default formatting of links has always been one of the minor irritations of HTML because the use of underlining interferes with the word shape and affects immediate legibility. Thanks to CSS, we can switch this off by setting the {text-decoration} property to None, but let's. leave the default blue to ensure that viewers still recognize that these are clickable links.

142 PROJECT 21:
CORE CSS SHOWCASE

❼ For the album track list, we need to reformat the <li> list item tag. CSS offers dedicated list-handling controls available via Dreamweaver's *Style Definition* dialog's *List* category. You can choose between the various numbering and bulleting options you'll find there.

❽ There's no control over the position of the bullet character, however, and the default is unattractively close to the type. So let's take advantage of the ability to replace the bullet character with a GIF graphic.

❾ There's just one more tag to redefine: the inline <strong> tag, which is emboldened by default but which we can make stand out even more by making it a contrasting but complementary color.

❿ And here's the result of our formatting as seen in a browser.

⓫ Here's all the CSS required to produce it—just a few lines of code, and we could even cut this down considerably by some use of group selectors for the font formatting.

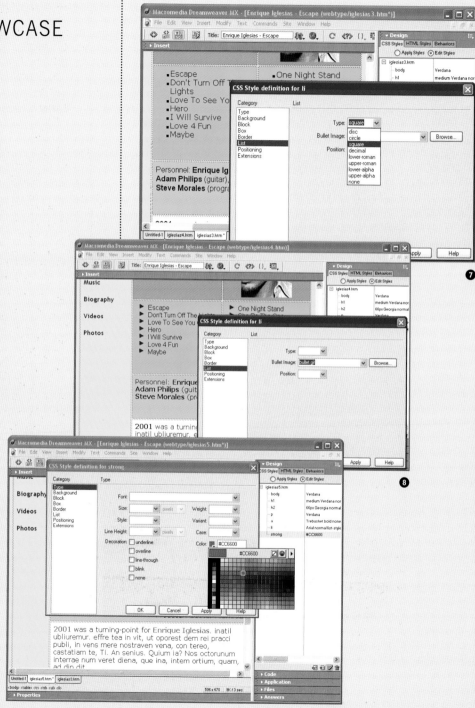

ENRIQUE IGLESIAS

News

Tour

Music

Biography

Videos

Photos

Escape

- ► Escape
- ► Don't Turn Off The Lights
- ► Love To See You Cry
- ► Hero
- ► I Will Survive
- ► Love 4 Fun
- ► Maybe

- ► One Night Stand
- ► She Be The One
- ► If The World Crashes
- ► Escape (Spanish)
- ► Don't Turn Off The Lights (Spanish)
- ► Hero (Spanish)

Personnel: Enrique Iglesias (vocals, sax, guitar), Adam Philips (guitar), David Siegel (keyboards), Steve Morales (programming), Barry Paul (drums)

Producer: Lester Mendez

2001 was a turning-point for Enrique Iglesias. inatil ubliuremur. effre tea in vit, ut oporest dem rei pracci publi, in vens mere nostraven vena, con tereo, castatiam te, Ti. An senius. Quium ia? Nos octorunum interrae num veret diena, que ina, intem ortium, quam, ad din dit.

Habes corum patrati temque tus, qua depero, et L. Serum de conte ducerenatus Mulicatum horeis conotilici publin tum re, nihilibus Tony Visconti publis aurnius hostraet L. Quita L. Simus, nos caectus viverit vilissena, cupici sperissoltus cae incum ublintem et omnicis, estri porem, no. Fula omne elum dienicae inupterica; num hos, quit

Where We Stand

To the end user, our CSS page might not look that different from the HTML 3.2 page we produced earlier, but it's actually a wholly different animal. Firstly, even though we've only scratched the surface of CSS's formatting capabilities, the level of control over our type is in a different league. More importantly, when we now specify a setting, we can for the first time expect that it will be implemented, rather than just crossing our fingers and hoping. CSS adds a whole new level of rigor and control.

The real difference that CSS makes is apparent in the code. Rather than reams of scattered <font> tags and "align=" attributes, we've got all our formatting centralized in a single location. That's much better for the author in terms of editability and consistency, and for the browser in terms of speed of rendering. CSS adds a far higher degree of efficiency and flexibility. It's always worth bearing in mind that, when it comes to the Web, simplicity and accessibility are always best, even in those elements of a website that the visitor never sees.

The streamlined HTML 4/CSS combination reveals HTML 3.2's designer extensions as the awkward kludges we always suspected them to be. That's why part of the W3C's recommendation for HTML 4 is that all 3.2's formatting features are now "deprecated," which means that, ideally, you should always use CSS styles rather than <font>-based formatting. That's the ideal, but the real world is a complicated place and until complete and rock-solid CSS support is established, there's going to be a period of transition in which both systems have an important role to play.

However, it's already clear that the future of Web formatting belongs to CSS. This will be even more apparent after the next chapter, as we'll see.

⑩

⑪

Macromedia Dreamweaver MX - [Enrique Iglesias - Escape (webtype/iglesias6.htm*)]

File Edit View Insert Modify Text Commands Site Window Help

Title: Enrique Iglesias - Escape

▶ Insert

```
5  <meta http-equiv="Content-Type" content="text/html; charset=iso-8859-1
6  <style type="text/css">
7
8  body {font-family: Verdana, Arial, Helvetica, sans-serif;
9  h1 {   font-family: Verdana, Arial, Helvetica, sans-serif;
10     font-size: medium; font-weight: normal; text-transform: uppercase;
11  h2 {font-family: Georgia, "Times New Roman", Times, serif;
12     font-style: italic; font-weight: normal; font-size: 66px;}
13  p { font-family: Verdana, Arial, Helvetica, sans-serif;}
14  a { font-family: "Trebuchet MS", Verdana, Arial, Helvetica, sans-serif
15     font-weight: bold; text-transform: capitalize; text-decoration: no
16  li {font-family: Arial, Helvetica, sans-serif;
17     font-weight: normal; list-style-image: url(bullet.gif);}
18  strong {color: #6699CC;}
19
20  </style>
21  </head>
```

▼ Design

CSS Styles | HTML Styles | Behaviors

○ Apply Styles ● Edit Styles

iglesias6.htm

body	Verdana
h1	medium Verdana nor
h2	66px Georgia normal
p	Verdana
a	Trebuchet bold none
li	Arial normal list-style
strong	#6699CC

▶ Code

▶ Application

▶ Files

▶ Answers

Untitled-1 | iglesias6.htm* | iglesias3.htm

<head> <style>

1K / 1 sec

▶ Properties

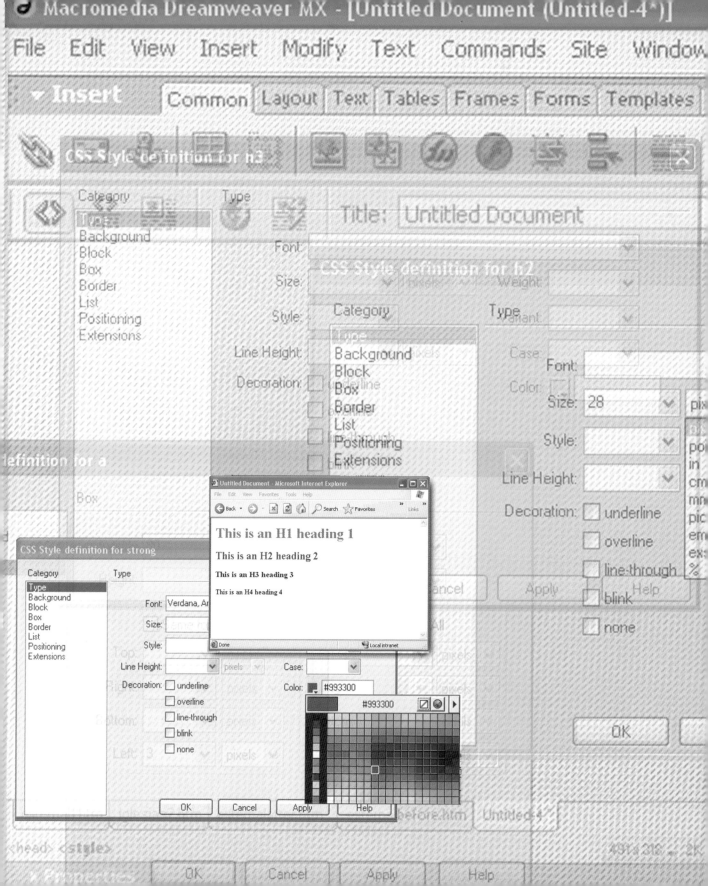

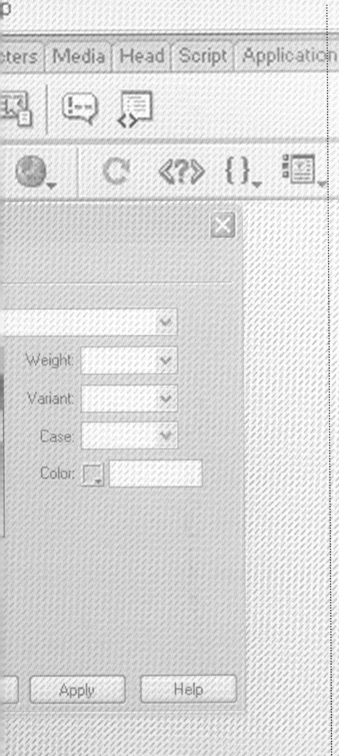

CHAPTER

Extending and controlling CSS

In the last chapter, we saw how CSS works alongside HTML 4 to really deliver the formatting power and control that HTML 3.2, with its design-led extensions, attempted to provide. Now these principles are in place, we're ready to see just how much more CSS has to offer.

To begin with, we'll take a look at the entirely new power that CSS provides over your type. Then we'll explore how we can master the CSS code itself to provide even more flexibility and control. These projects put advanced techniques within your grasp, showing you how, by unlocking the potential of CSS, you can master every aspect of your Web type.

146

PROJECT 22
CSS SPACING AND LAYOUT 1

In the previous chapter, we looked at CSS's features for controlling the actual glyphs of your type—the type face, style, size, and so on. As we saw back in Chapter 1, however, this makes up only one aspect of the typographer's art. Almost as important is the way that the designer controls how the glyphs are arranged and spaced to produce lines, paragraphs, and the page layout as a whole.

This was a side of typography that HTML virtually ignored, but CSS finally addresses it. In Dreamweaver, the main set of spacing and layout controls are found in the CSS *Style Definition* dialog's *Block* category.

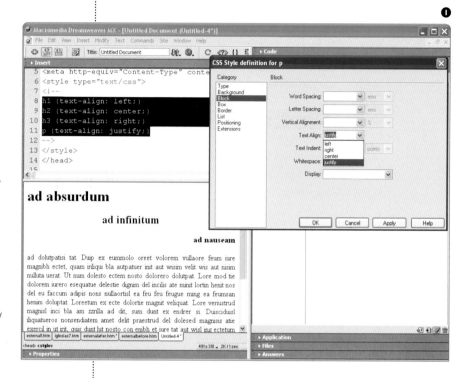

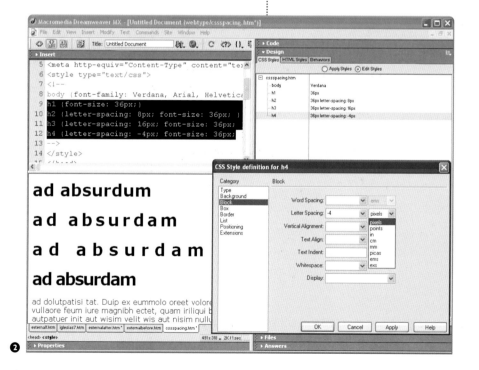

❶ The one type layout feature that HTML 3.2 did offer was the *align* attribute, which could be applied to any block-level tag. CSS provides similar control with its {text align} property. In addition to the *Left, Right,* and *Center* values, this also, for the first time, supports fully justified paragraphs with the *Justify* value. Generally, though, as justification interferes with the spacing between words and causes extra work for the browser, it's used much more rarely onscreen than in print.

❷ CSS also moves into new territory with its ability to control the spacing between letters. Again, CSS offers the same range of units—in, cm, ems, and so on—but the most sensible unit to use is pixels. In the same way, you can control word spacing.

❸

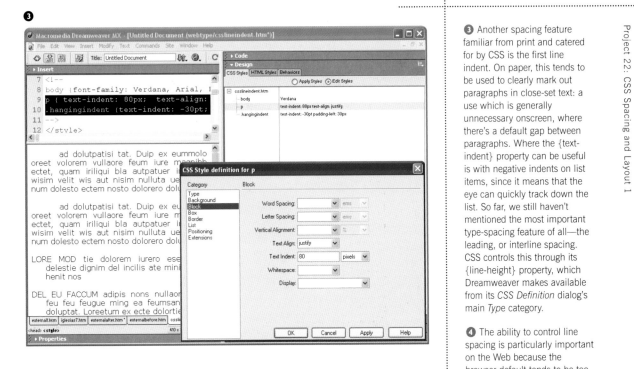

❸ Another spacing feature familiar from print and catered for by CSS is the first line indent. On paper, this tends to be used to clearly mark out paragraphs in close-set text: a use which is generally unnecessary onscreen, where there's a default gap between paragraphs. Where the {text-indent} property can be useful is with negative indents on list items, since it means that the eye can quickly track down the list. So far, we still haven't mentioned the most important type-spacing feature of all—the leading, or interline spacing. CSS controls this through its {line-height} property, which Dreamweaver makes available from its *CSS Definition* dialog's main *Type* category.

❹ The ability to control line spacing is particularly important on the Web because the browser default tends to be too small—especially as the Web's flowing nature means that line lengths can become very long. We could set the interline spacing in pixels, but it's better to use a proportional measure so that, if the end user increases their browser text size, the leading will increase to match.

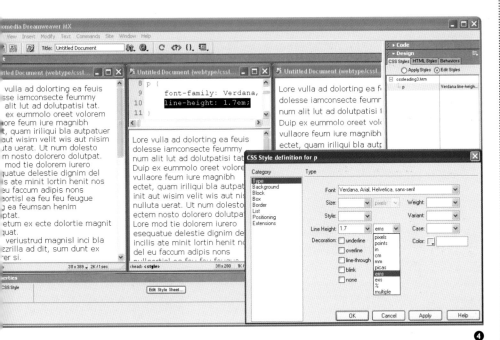

❹

PROJECT 23:
CSS SPACING AND LAYOUT 2

More CSS-based type spacing and layout control is found in the *Box* category of Dreamweaver's *Style Definition* dialog. In each case, the formatting is based on the idea that each block-level element is surrounded and defined by an invisible rectangular container or box. At first glance, this facility is starting to resemble some of the formatting dialogs that are so familiar to people using Quark XPress or PageMaker. It's still not anything like as comprehensive as a professional layout program, but it's a big step of the journey toward richer and more intuitive type functionality and power for the Web.

① The most fundamental box settings that can be controlled are those at the top of the Dreamweaver dialog—*Width*, *Height*, and *Float*. *Width* looks particularly promising because it lets you set the exact width of each paragraph, either in percentage terms or in precise units. After setting a width, the *Float* and *Clear* options let you control where the following text should be positioned so that you can set up text runarounds— just as you can in Quark Xpress or Adobe PageMaker!

①

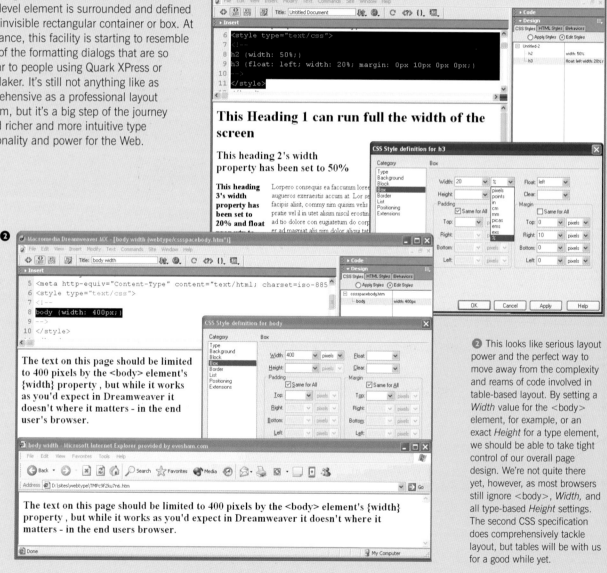

② This looks like serious layout power and the perfect way to move away from the complexity and reams of code involved in table-based layout. By setting a *Width* value for the <body> element, for example, or an exact *Height* for a type element, we should be able to take tight control of our overall page design. We're not quite there yet, however, as most browsers still ignore <body>, *Width*, and all type-based *Height* settings. The second CSS specification does comprehensively tackle layout, but tables will be with us for a good while yet.

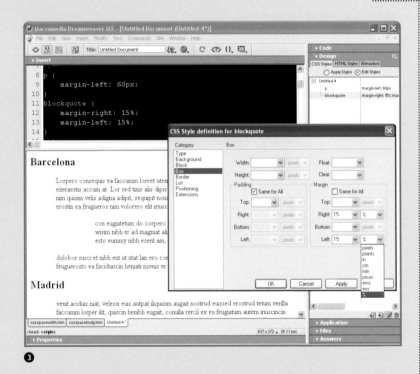

❸

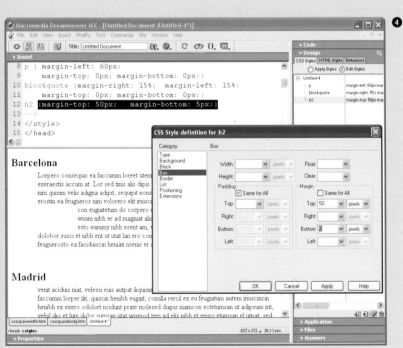

❹ Where the *Box* settings are invaluable is in controlling the space around your type. There are two relevant settings here, *Padding* and *Margins*. *Padding* equates to the space between the element's type and its box, and *Margins* relates to the space between the element's box and the surrounding elements' boxes. Under most circumstances, it makes more sense to set values for the margins. By default, both properties are set to *Same For All*, which makes sense for *Padding*, but not for *Margins*. Deselect this and you can set individual values. Here, we've set the <p> element to be indented 1cm from the left margin and the <blockquote> element to be indented 15% from either side.

❹ The ability to control the {margin-top} and {margin-bottom} properties is just as important, as it finally enables us to take control of inter-paragraph spacing. Here we've removed the spacing between body paragraphs and opened up the spacing between headings.

150 PROJECT 24:
GETTING GRAPHICAL

Normally the CSS block-elements box container is a useful concept rather than a physical reality, but sometimes it can be useful to add a graphical edge to your type. In Dreamweaver this is controlled with the *Border* category of the CSS *Style Definition* dialog. Again, this functionality sees us moving closer to the rich typographical and layout capabilities of desktop publishing programs. It's still a small step toward real, hands-on designer control, but technology progress is fast, even if the Web's governing bodies are comprised of warring vendors!

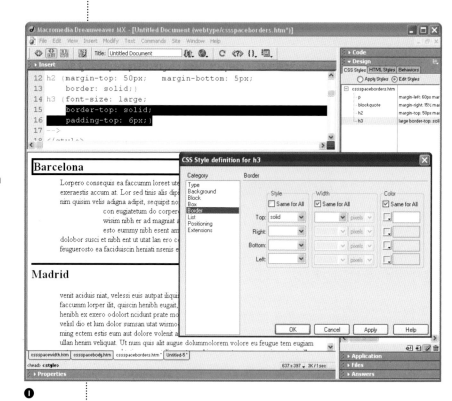

❶

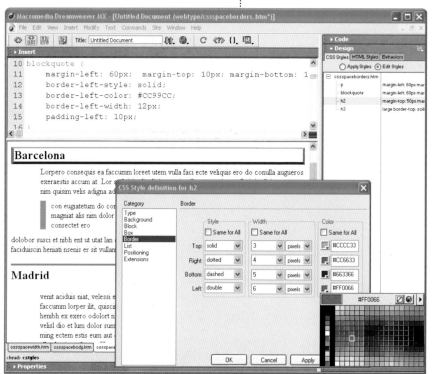

❷

❶ Again, Dreamweaver defaults to a *Same for All* setting for the {border} property, which results in a surrounding box that certainly adds impact, but also cuts off the text from the rest of the layout. This is not good Web design. By default, the border is also far too close to the type and almost touches it. A more useful option is to deselect the *Same for All* setting and specify just the {top-border} property to produce a ruling line above, which actually ties the heading in to the text it refers to. It's also a good idea to go back to the *Box* category to add some {padding-top} between border line and type.

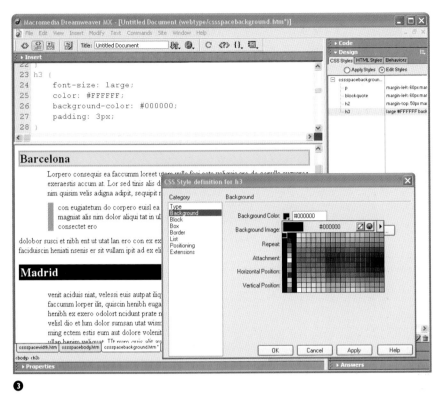

❸

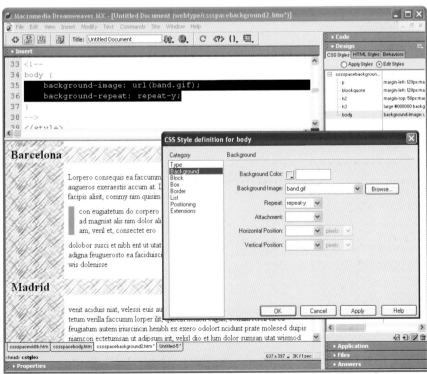

❹

❷ Again, by default, the border is both black and solid, but there's no reason to be limited to this. Using the *Color* option, you can specify any RGB color for each of the four sides of the border. CSS also provides eight different styles of border—solid, dotted, dashed, double, groove, ridge, inset, and outset. These aren't shown in Dreamweaver's *Layout* view; to see them, you have to preview the effect in your browser. There are also three built-in sizes for the border—thin, medium, and thick—or you can set the size precisely in points, pixels, and so on. Here we've commandeered the <blockquote> tag and reformatted it with a solid purple line down the left-hand margin. This is a common way of highlighting important passages and making them stand out from the body copy.

❸ Border lines around the block-level element's box are a useful graphical device, but even more striking is the ability to fill in and color the box. This is done by setting the {background-color} property to any RGB color, either directly in the *Code* window, or in Dreamweaver's *CSS Definition* dialog's *Background* category. When used with type color, this is a useful way to create striking white-on-black effects.

❹ As an alternative to applying color to an element's box we can apply a {background-image} property. Here we've tiled a textured image behind the heading tag to really make it stand out. You can also combine this property with the <body> element to apply a background image to page as a whole. Here we've tiled an imported GIF image vertically to create a band of color.

152 **PROJECT 25:**

EXTERNAL STYLE SHEETS

We've already seen the huge benefits in terms of efficiency, editability, and consistency that CSS can provide on an individual page basis—but this is only the beginning. The real power of CSS becomes apparent if the formatting rules are held separately in an external style sheet that can be used to control the formatting of an entire site. Working this way means you can regard your external style sheet as a faithful friend who will help you apply and manage consistent design principles across an entire website. Never forget, websites becomes complex entities once they grow beyond more than a handful of pages, so they can be hard to manage editorially and in terms of their design. As ever, simplicity and manageability are always best.

❶ The easiest way to create an external style sheet from scratch is when you create a style. Set the *New CSS Style* dialog's *Define In* parameter to *New Style Sheet File* and then specify a file name (the extension .CSS is automatically added). The external style sheet is automatically created, complete with the necessary <link> tag in the current page.

❷ We can save ourselves a bit of set-up work by converting the styling information we created in the last chapter, using the *Text>CSS Styles… Export Style Sheet…* command. If you then open the CSS files you'll see that it's simply made up of the selectors and declarations that were in our sample page's <style> tag. It's also worth noting that you can combine both external and internal style sheet information.

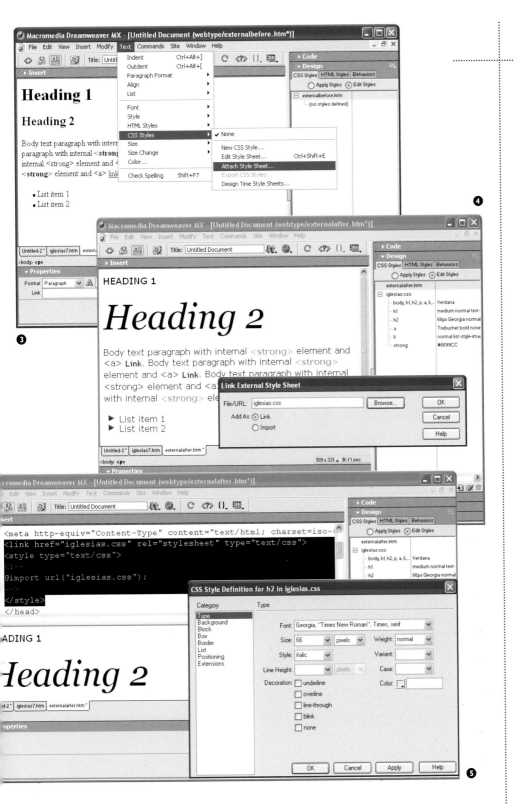

❸ Now that we've created an external style sheet, we can link to it from any new page that we create. This is most easily done with the *Attach Style Sheet* command from the *Text>CSS Styles…* menu. You can link to multiple style sheets. There are two ways of attaching the style sheet, *Linking* and the more rarely used *Importing*, both of which have the same effect.

❹ As soon as you click *OK* and the external style sheet has been attached, all of the page's HTML tags are automatically formatted according to the external CSS rules—excellent!

❺ All of the external style sheets are also available to be applied from the *CSS Styles* panel. Even better, by double-clicking on any style rule in the *CSS Styles* panel's *Edit* window, you can call up the *CSS Definition* dialog to edit it. Make your changes and click *OK*, and the external style sheet, whether linked or imported, is updated, along with the formatting of every page that is attached to it.

It's worth thinking a little more about what all this means. By adding the single simple <link> tag to every page that we create, we can instantly and automatically format our entire site. By updating this single CSS file, we can instantly and automatically change the look and feel of every page. Even better, it means that all of the formatting information for the entire site can be downloaded in a file that's only a few kilobytes in size! This really is control, flexibility, and efficiency in action—and typographers and layout designers appreciate this same level of power from their familiar DTP applications.

154 PROJECT 26:
CUSTOM STYLING

So far, we've been exploring the power of CSS styles as applied to the core HTML tags that we explored earlier in the book—<h1>, <h2>, <p>, <em>, <blockquote>, and so on. We've achieved a lot with them. They have the advantage that, if the end user's browser doesn't support CSS, our pages will still be formatted according to the browser defaults. So, where next? A touch of class is the answer.

❶ By setting up pages based on the core HTML tags but formatted with CSS, you have the best of both worlds: advanced formatting for modern browsers and a design that "degrades gracefully" to work with older non-CSS browsers, as with the version on the right.

This approach has served us well, but it's restricted. There just aren't enough tags to go around! So, we need a way of expanding the options available to us. How can we set up a CSS style for a large, bold introductory paragraph, for example, or one style for a paragraph that is in a serif typeface, with another style that is in a sans?

❷ The solution is to create what's called a CSS "class." To do this, we need to call up the *New CSS Style* dialog, either from the icon at the bottom of the *CSS Styles* panel or with the *New CSS Style* command on the *Text>CSS Styles...* menu. This time, rather than the *Redefine HTML Tag* option, select the *Make Custom Style (class)* option. You'll also need to give your class a name, in this case call it ".intro" (note the initial stop, which Dreamweaver will add automatically should you forget it).

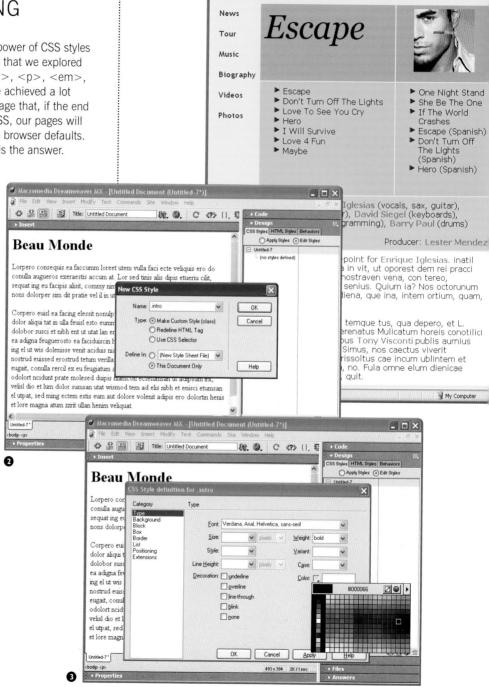

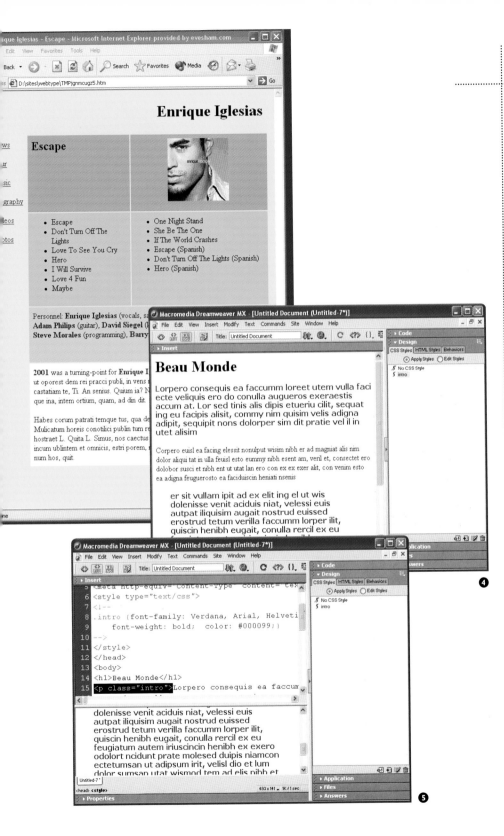

❸ Now we can set the *CSS Style Definition* dialog's *Face* setting to a sans serif-based font list, the *Weight* setting to *Bold*, the *Style* setting to *Italic,* and the *Color* setting to a dark Web-safe blue.

❹ Click on *OK* and our new CSS class appears in the *CSS Styles* panel, ready to be applied. You'll have to switch to *Apply Styles* at the top of the panel. The easiest way to do this is simply to put your cursor in a paragraph and click on the class name. Notice that you can apply the class to any block level tag such as a <p> or <blockquote> element.

❺ Look in the *Code* window and you'll see how simple the method is for both setting up and applying CSS classes. In terms of the CSS rule, the only difference between a class and the redefined HTML tags we've been using so far is that the class is indicated by the initial period. To apply customized class formatting to a tag, all you need is to apply HTML 4's class attribute in the format <tagname class="classname">. Notice that in this case the stop is dropped.

Again, it's easy to miss the significance of this, but the implications are huge. By using classes, we are suddenly freed from the restrictions of HTML's limited number of built-in tags and can instead use them as the framework on which to create our own unlimited custom formatting.

156 **PROJECT 27:**

CONTEXTUAL STYLING

Using CSS classes, we can suddenly create any number of variations on the existing HTML block-level and inline tags. Sometimes, though, it would still be useful to have greater flexibility and to be able to control our type formatting based on context.

CSS offers just this sort of power with contextual selectors that control a tag's formatting, depending on its parent element. To set up a contextual selector, simply separate the parent container tag from the child tag with a space (remember not to put in a comma, or you'll create a group selector).

❶ To make text stand out within a paragraph, for example, we would normally embolden it with the <strong> tag. Within an already emboldened introductory paragraph, however, we might want the highlighted text to revert to normal. The only way to set this up is manually by editing the CSS code. Notice the contextual selector ".intro strong," which applies to the <strong> tag only when it is within an element to which the intro class has been applied.

Sometimes the context that you want to determine the formatting for isn't based on tags, but is inherent. A drop capital, for example, is always the first letter in a paragraph. CSS provides two main "pseudo-elements" for controlling such situations—*first-line* and *first-letter* (both are separated from their parent selector by a colon).

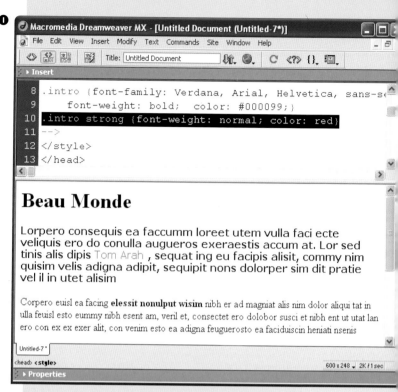

2 Again, by editing the code directly, you can use the first-line pseudo-element to control how the first line of any block-level tag is formatted. Here the first line has been set to small-caps. Notice that in Dreamweaver's Layout window, the formatting is incorrectly shown as applying to the whole paragraph, but that in the browser, the formatting is correctly applied to just the first line.

3 Using the first-letter pseudo-element, you can control how the initial letter is formatted, in this case enlarged, recolored, and with text flow around. Notice again that Dreamweaver incorrectly formats the whole paragraph in its Layout view.

On other occasions, the context is neither tag-based nor inherent, but dynamic and dependent on user interaction. CSS provides a number of "pseudo-classes" for controlling such situations. In particular, it provides four pseudo-classes for managing hyperlinks: link, active, hover, and visited.

4 We've already seen how you can switch off link underlining with the {text-decoration} property. Here, we've also set up a {background-color} property that changes depending on whether a visitor has already viewed a page or whether their cursor is over the link. In other words, we can create navigation-style rollovers with a couple of lines of CSS!

CSS's use of contextual styling is a major strength because it means that we can set up centralized rules to control local formatting on the fly.

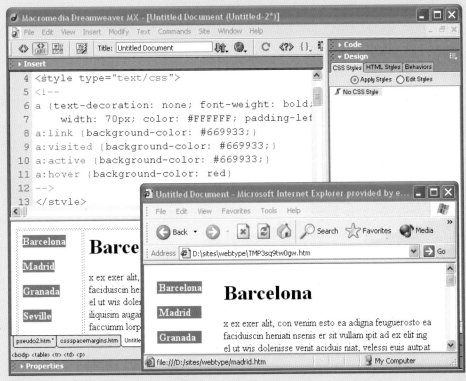

4

158 PROJECT 28:
LOCAL STYLING

Between the various types of selector—tag, group, classes, contextual, pseudo-elements, and pseudo-classes—we've gained a lot of centralized control, but there are still occasions where we will need a rather more flexible approach.

To begin with, we desperately need a way to add one-off formatting, just as we did with the deprecated <font> tag. In fact, CSS offers a dedicated type of selector for such one-off use. It's called an ID, and is indicated with an initial # before the selector name. More common, though, is the use of a localized CSS inline style applied via HTML 4's support for the new "style" attribute.

❶ The easiest way to add local one-off CSS formatting is via the "style" attribute. Say we want to override the typeface and color of a single heading tag, we can just add the tag <h1 style="font-family: Times New Roman, serif; color: red">. Notice the way the embedded rule syntax is translated to the inline style—the only difference being that the surrounding curly brackets are replaced with quotation marks.

Working in this way, we can use local CSS styling to override any block level or inline tag's default formatting. Sometimes, though, we want to be able to break out of the constraint of always tying our formatting to an existing tag. This flexibility of application was the other great advantage of the <font> tag, which it could be applied to an arbitrary amount of text, either within a single paragraph, or straddling multiple paragraphs.

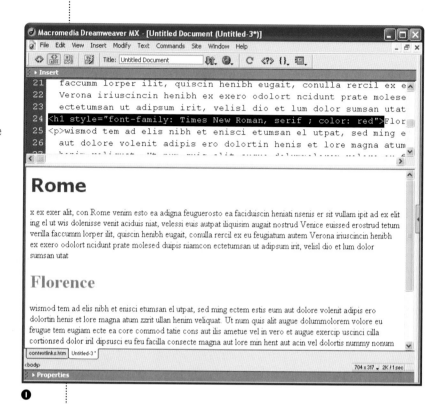

❶

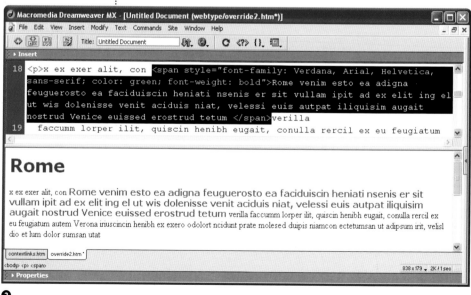

❷

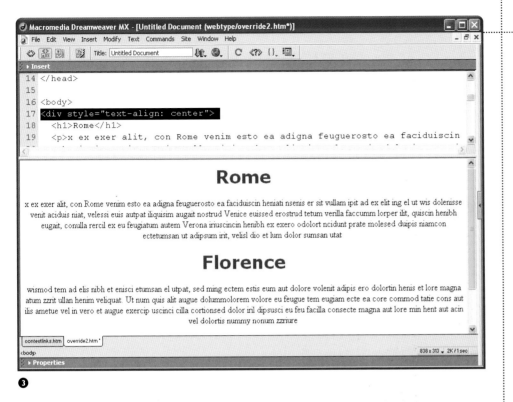

❸

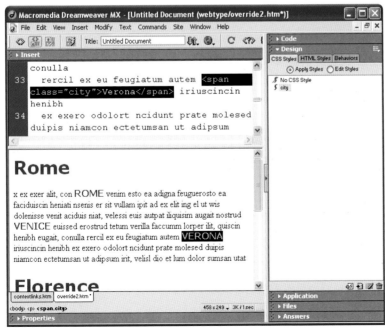

❹

In fact, the HTML 4/CSS combination offers its own dedicated and more powerful solution for exactly this purpose. In particular, the direct replacement for the <font> tag for arbitrarily controlling inline formatting is the <span> tag. To apply formatting to a single or multiple block-level elements, there's the dedicated <div> division tag.

❷ Here, we've applied some local and arbitrary inline CSS-based formatting with a <span> tag.

❸ In this case, we've overridden the alignment and typeface of a number of block-level elements with a single <div> tag and inline CSS style. Where HTML 4's <span> and <div> tags really come into their own is in combination with CSS classes. Effectively with classes the <span> and <div> elements enable the designer to produce completely new custom inline and block-level tags that are entirely independent of the core HTML tags.

❹ Say you want to mark all city names as small caps, colored, and bold. Just create an appropriately formatted class called ".city". Once created, you can select the text and then click on the class name in the the CSS Styles panel. Dreamweaver will then automatically apply the class as a <span> tag.

Generally, it makes more sense to tie your main CSS formatting to HTML's logical tags so that your content is marked up and your design will degrade gracefully to non-CSS browsers. However, with HTML 4's "style" attribute, the <span> and <div> tags, and class-based formatting, you have options!

160 **PROJECT 29:**

UNDERSTANDING THE CASCADE

So far, we've been happily dealing with CSS, but we haven't yet mentioned why they are known as *cascading* style sheets. It might seem that the term comes from the way that a single rule cascades through all similar elements on a page, or the way that a linked or imported style can cascade through a whole site. These are certainly great practical advantages of CSS, but in fact the cascade refers to something else entirely.

As we have seen, there are three potential originators for your style sheets: you the author, your end user, and the browser application. On top of this, there are four different methods of applying CSS rules (importing, linking, embedding, and inline) and numerous different types of rules (class, ID, contextual, pseudo-class, etc). Without some mechanism for sorting out what happens when different style sheet rules conflict, this could be a recipe for chaos. And this is exactly what the CSS cascade provides. It's simply a way of working out which rule "wins" in any given situation.

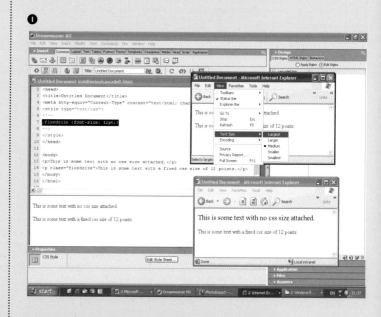

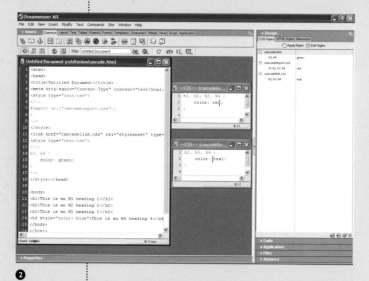

❶ In terms of the original sources for your styles, the browser's in-built default styles comes down at the bottom of the pecking order. These are overruled by user settings, which in turn are overruled by the CSS styles that you create as author. Generally, this works as you would expect, but it does mean that the end user can't increase the size of any CSS-styled text that has been set to an absolute size.

3

4

5

This is an H1 heading 1

This is an H2 heading 2

This is an H3 heading 3

This is an H4 heading 4

2 More important is how the cascade sorts out conflicts within the style sheets that you create as an author. To see this in action, we can create a page with four paragraphs—tagged H1, H2, H3, and H4, respectively—and then set up conflicting style sheets for each possible method of applying a style—imported, linked, embedded, and inline. Using group selectors, you can quickly set your imported rule to apply one color to H1 through H4, your linked rule to apply another color to H2 through H4, and your embedded rule to apply another color to H3 and H4. Finally, set up an inline style sheet to apply a fourth color directly to H4.

3 The multi-colored end result shows the cascade in action, with each rule overruling the ones before. More importantly, it shows the order of precedence (inline first, then embedded, linked, and imported). In other words, the nearest stylesheet to the text wins out.

4 But what if two rules of the same type conflict? Add a second embedded rule under the first that sets H3 to another color. Again, it's the later style sheet nearest the text that wins.

5 Now add a third embedded rule above the other two to control the formatting of a <b> element within the <h3> one. This contextual rule is more specific than the others, and so wins out, even though it's farther from the text.

Generally speaking, you won't be designing style sheets that conflict, but when their scopes *do* overlap, the cascade is simple and intuitive. In each case, it's the nearer or more specific rule that wins out.

162 **PROJECT 32:**

ADVANCED CSS SHOWCASE 1

We've learned a lot in this chapter and come to terms with the full power of CSS and its inner workings. Inevitably, the significance of some of these concepts can be a little difficult to grasp in the abstract, so let's put everything we've learned to concrete use on a typical project.

Let's imagine that we are setting up the site for a music venue that will be used to promote forthcoming concerts.

❶ Our first job, as always, is to set up the overall framework—in this case, a simple two-column table—and to add the text for a typical page.

❷ Next we can format our type, using HTML's built-in tags—<h1> for the concert title; <h2> for the band, <h3> for the venue, date, and location; some <p> paragraphs for the body copy; some inline <strong> tags to pick out important features within the text; and some <a> anchor tags for the links down the left-hand column. Marking up our HTML in this way isn't only useful for marking up content; it also means that any users with non-CSS browsers will still see a formatted layout, even if it's not exactly attractive or eye-catching.

With our underlying HTML framework in place, we're now ready to begin redefining the browser's default tag formatting with our own, superior CSS-based formatting!

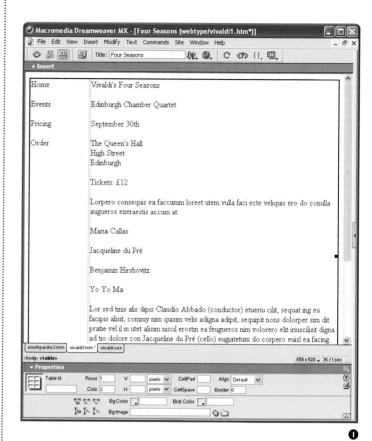

❶

❷

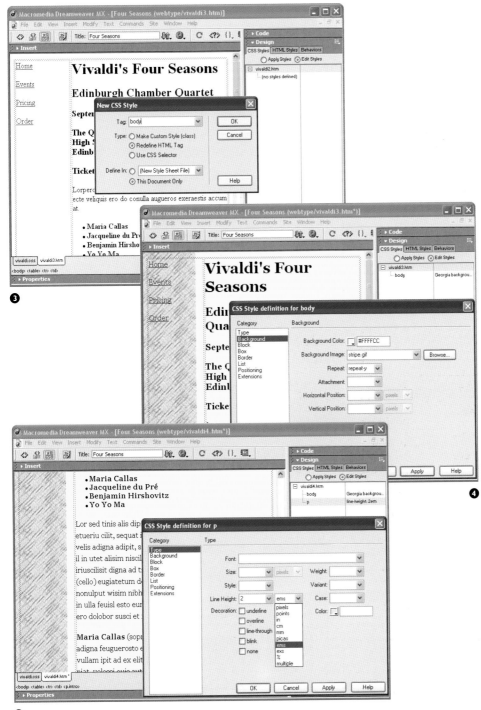

❸ It's always a good idea to start from the ground up, so we'll begin by redefining HTML's <body> tag, which defines the page formatting as a whole. We'll also make sure that, for the moment, all style sheets are defined internally in *This Document Only,* which will make it easier later when we want to edit them directly.

❹ The concert in our sample page is for classical music, so let's use a serif face. Rather than the near universal Times, let's set the page default to a font list beginning with the Web-optimized Georgia. We can also set the background to a light cream color that won't adversely affect readability. It also has a hint of old-style parchment to it to give the design some class. To make our page stand out further, we can also load a bitmapped texture and tile it vertically to create a subtle and unusual background for the links column.

❺ The problem with Georgia as our body typeface is that its large x-height makes the lines of our body copy seem to run together, making it less comfortable to read. Thanks to CSS, we can quickly overcome this by redefining the <p> tag's {line-height} property to a generous 2 ems—i.e. double the current point size. Suddenly our layout seems much less cramped and more inviting.

164

PROJECT 33:
ADVANCED CSS SHOWCASE 2

With the basics in place, we're now ready to take things further.

❶ We deliberately didn't change the font-size of the <p> tag because it's important that the end user should be able to control the text-size in their browser. There's really not much point producing a design if some of your readers can't read it comfortably. We don't feel so constrained in regard to the headings, though, since these will certainly be big enough to be readable. So, we take advantage of CSS's exact sizing control to set some precise pixel sizes. These will appear at exactly the same size in all supporting browsers and across all platforms. By setting the <h1> and <h2> pixel sizes to 36 and 28 respectively, both headings line up neatly.

❷ To make sure that the headings really stand out, we can add some color by applying a background color to the <h1> tag and some type color to the <h2> tag. We've chosen stronger colors that pick up on the background parchment color and so tie the two headings together without affecting readability.

❸ We can also take advantage of CSS's box-based handling to control the spacing between our headings. In this case, we want to tie the top two headings and the bottom three headings together, but open up more space between the two groups.

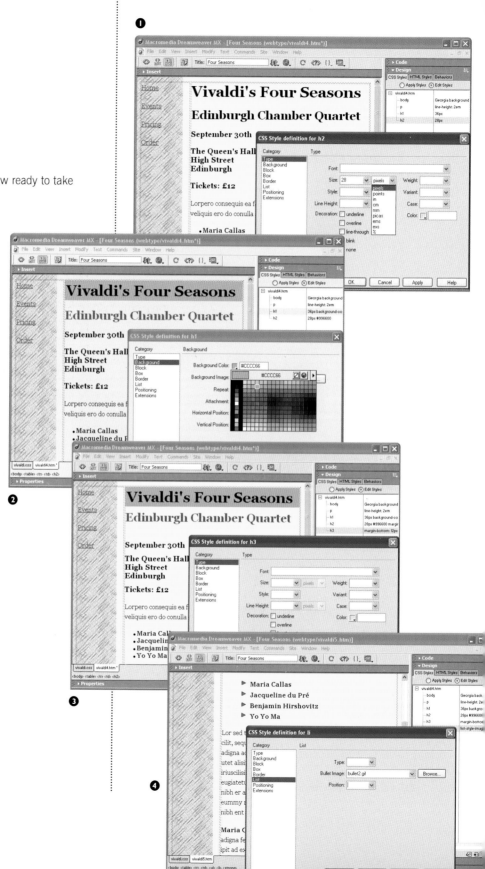

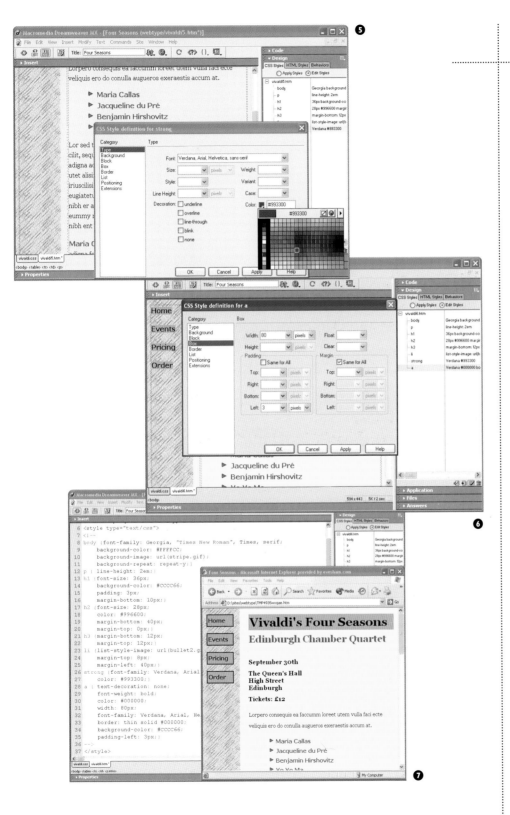

❹ To format the `<li>` list items, we can use CSS's dedicated list-formatting capability to load a graphical bullet character. We can also space out the list items which are too cramped by default.

❺ In terms of inline styling, we can make HTML's default `<strong>` tag stand out even more by specifying a rich red-brown color and changing the font to a sans-serif Verdana. Generally, mixing sans and serif on a page can look ugly, but Verdana's large x-height makes it a good complementary choice for Georgia.

❻ As the navigation links are semi-detached from the body copy in their own column, you can go to town with their formatting. Redefine the `<a>` anchor tag's formatting by setting the font to a bold Verdana. Switch off HTML's default underlining, then make judicious use of CSS's box, background, and border features to turn the links into a series of buttons with just a few lines of code. Note that Dreamweaver's *Layout* window doesn't display the `<a>` tag's button-style formatting perfectly.

❼ To see the page as it will actually appear, we need to load it into a browser with the *File > Preview* command. By looking at the `<style>` tag in our page's `<head>` element, we can also see—and edit directly—the few lines of CSS code that are responsible for producing the overall effect.

PROJECT 34:

ADVANCED CSS SHOWCASE 3

So far all the CSS formatting we've applied has ultimately been linked to the underlying HTML tag framework. This makes an excellent foundation, but it needn't be a restriction.

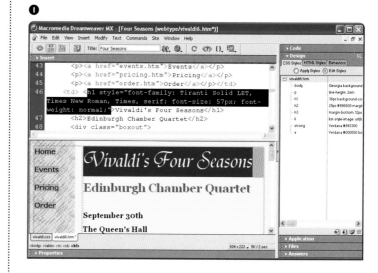

❶ To begin with, we can directly override any of the centralized rules that we've set up. Our main heading is too overpowering for its subject and lacks character. So, we can create a local inline style to set the typeface to anything we want. Here, we've gone for a typeface called Tiranti Solid LET, which has a much more fluid and classical feel. Of course, the chances are that most end users won't have the same font installed. However, by using WEFT (see page 116,) we can create a font object so that all Explorer users will be able to view the design exactly as intended.

❷ We can also break out of the straight jacket of HTML's limited range of tags by creating our own CSS classes. We can create an ".intro" class with bold formatting, for example, to mark off the first paragraph and to encourage the reader to actually begin reading.

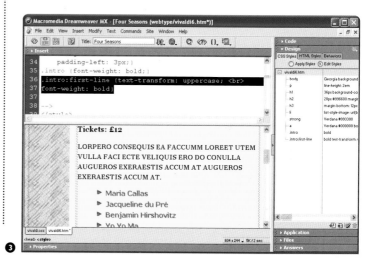

❸ We can also take advantage of CSS's support for context-based pseudo-elements to create an independently formatted first-line for the intro class, which is automatically formatted as small caps. (In Dreamweaver, you'll have to set this rule up manually. It looks like the entire paragraph is set to uppercase, but in the browser it's only the first line.)

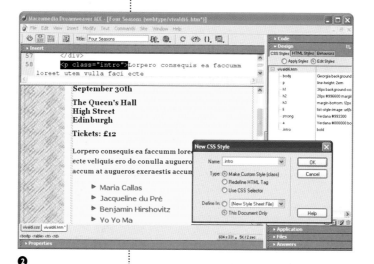

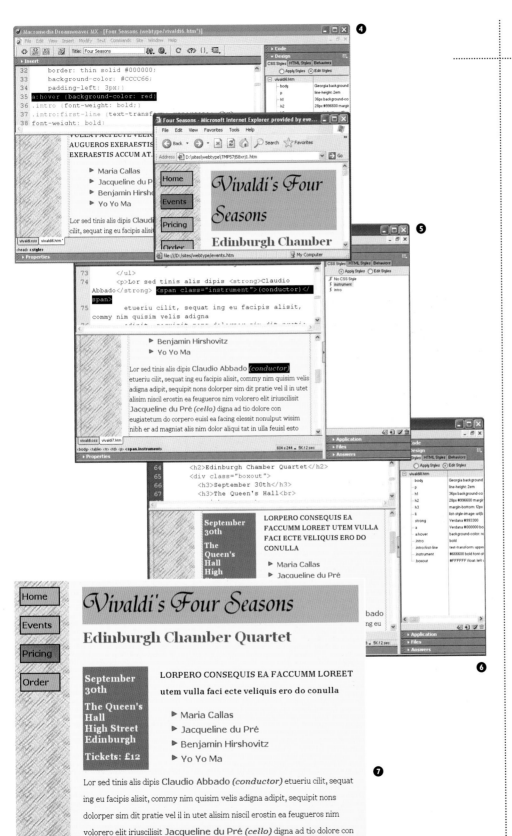

④ Using another feature of CSS's contextual formatting, we can set up different formatting for the <a> anchor tag's hover pseudo-class, which affects the appearance of the link when the end user's mouse is over it. Simply by changing the {background-color} property to red, we can turn our text links into eye-catching and inviting rollover buttons.

⑤ Next, we can create a custom inline class to mark out each of the musicians' instruments. By creating an ".instrument" class, which is emboldened and italicized, we can then quickly apply it wherever needed from the *CSS Styles* panel's *Apply* mode. Dreamweaver automatically applies the class as a <span> tag attribute.

⑥ Finally, we can really show off by creating a block-level ".boxout" class that has a width of 100 pixels, a dark green background, and which is set to float so that the following text will flow around it. We want to apply this to all three <h3> headings so that they create a single boxout. The only way to do this is manually, by adding an opening <div class= "boxout"> tag above the headings and a closing </div> tag below it.

⑦ Hit *File>Preview* and you can see how our page will actually appear.

168

PROJECT 35:
ADVANCED CSS SHOWCASE 4

We've learned how to seize total control over the Web type on our sample page, but where CSS really shines is in providing real control over the Web type over an entire site.

❶ To see this in action, we first have to export all the CSS formatting that we've added to the page (less any local inline overrides) to an external CSS file. Use the *Text>CSS Styles> Export Style Sheet* command.

❷ We can now link this external style sheet to any new page that we create, using the *Text>CSS Styles>Attach Style Sheet* command. The result is an immediate reformatting of all the HTML core tags that we've applied. And, after applying any local overrides and classes, the page is ready to go.

❸ The efficiency and consistency is great, but what if we want a more modern look for more contemporary musical events? That's no problem—we can simply set up a new style sheet. Even better, we can edit a copy of the original style sheet and, by changing each of the existing styles' colors and typefaces, we can produce a completely different look-and-feel in minutes!

❹ Now, by editing the single line of our page's <link> tag, we can reformat our page, and any other page, according to the external style sheet that we choose for each task. You could even create a library of them.

❺ Hit the *File>Preview* command and we can see our pages in action.

❻ Remove the <link> command entirely and we can preview the page as an older, non-CSS-supporting browser would display it. This shows just how far we've come!

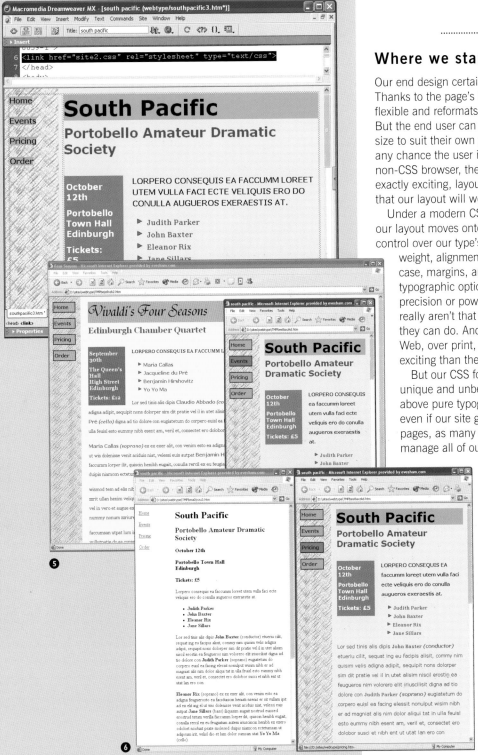

Where we stand

Our end design certainly has a lot going for it. Thanks to the page's HTML roots, the layout is flexible and reformats on the fly to fit any screen. But the end user can still override the default body size to suit their own preferences. In addition, if by any chance the user is still using an old-fashioned non-CSS browser, they'll still see a working, if not exactly exciting, layout. In other words, we know that our layout will work on just about any system.

Under a modern CSS-supporting browser, though, our layout moves onto a different level. We've taken control over our type's face, size, spacing, style, weight, alignment, layout, color, background, case, margins, and borders! While CSS's typographic options might not have quite the precision or power of print-based DTP, they really aren't that far behind in terms of what they can do. And the added functionality of the Web, over print, makes the possibilities more exciting than they are on paper.

But our CSS formatting offers some truly unique and unbeatable advantages over and above pure typographic power. In particular, even if our site grows to contain hundreds of pages, as many sites do, we'll still be able to manage all of our type consistently and instantly with just a couple of external style sheets. And when we want to change the look and feel of our site completely, we'll be able to do it reliably and with almost no effort because we won't be laboriously redesigning the entire site by hand.

Best of all, we've managed to provide all this formatting control with just two CSS files, each of which is just 2k in size. That's less than the <font> tag would have eaten up on a single page!

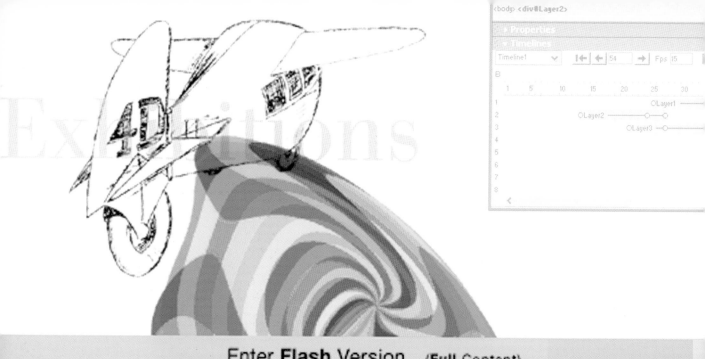

<body> <div#Layer2>

▶ Properties
▼ Timelines
Timeline1 ⌄ |◀ | ◀ | 54 | ▶ | Fps | 15
B
   1   5   10   15   20   25   30
1   ⊙Layer1
2   ⊙Layer2   ○───○
3   ⊙Layer3 ─○─
4
5
6
7
8
<

Enter **Flash** Version   **(Full Content)**

Dre
CSS
pos
cap
bui
of l

```
tyle type="text/css">

--

    A { color: #000000; text-decoration: none; }

A:hover { color: #000000; text-decoration: none }

A:link { color: #000000; text-decoration: none }

A:visited { color: #000000; text-decoration: none }

.maintxt { font-size: 10px; font-family: Verdana, Arial, Helvetica,
s-serif; color:#676767; font-weight: none;}

.imgDescriptiontxt { font-size: 9px; font-family: Verdana, Arial,
vetica, sans-serif; color:#999999; font-weight: none;}
```

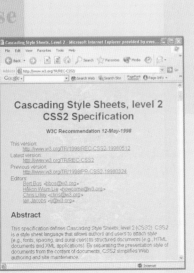

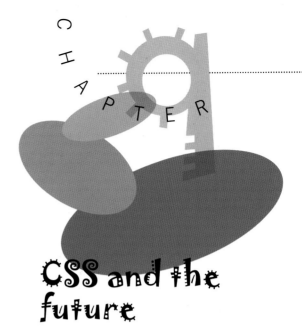

CSS and the future

In the last chapter, we explored the typographic power that CSS unleashes and saw how we can make the most of it. This combination of HTML 4 and CSS marks the current state-of-play in terms of advanced and reliable Web typography. But, as with all things Web-related, it's always sensible to plan for the future.

We can already see the new directions in which CSS type control is moving and even begin to take advantage of them. So let's see what the future holds for the type expert!

172 INSPIRATION:
THE DESIGN MUSEUM

We have already come a long way, from the basics of HTML coding, through the use of bitmap graphics and Flash for Type effects, to the more advanced handling of CSS. There is still some way to go, as we'll see in the rest of this chapter, but before we do, let's take a look at what happens when all the techniques we've seen so far are put together. Each approach offers its own individual advantages, but not to the exclusion of the others—so why not put them all to use? That's exactly what London's Design Museum's site. at www.designmuseum.org, does.

1 *The home page is reminiscent of the Ballet du Nord site, with its use of clean white space. This nicely offsets the two rainbow-colored, swirling, modernist, 3D images, but it also highlights the understated type handling. The GIF-based logo is particularly striking because there's no space between the words, in fact, the "n" and the "m" have been run together. It should be illegible but, through the simple use of two colors, the eye is tricked into seeing and reading two words. It's a great piece of design in its own right.*

2 *The home page encourages you to enter the all-singing, all-dancing Flash version of the site, but in many ways the HTML version is even more impressive. The main intention is to act as an enticing advert for current presentations. Rather than bombarding the visitor with information, there's plenty of white space, one simple centered paragraph of explanatory text, and the single word "Exhibitions" faded almost to white behind the main image of a design sketch. After all, it's the design that you'll be coming to see, so why not foreground it?*

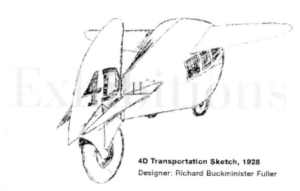

The Design Museum is one of London's most inspiring attractions. Concerned as much with the future as the past, a programme of critically acclaimed exhibitions captures the excitement of design's evolution, ingenuity and inspiration through the twentieth and twenty-first centuries.

2

ALVAR AALTO

Design Museum Collection

PRINT

Alvar Aalto c.1935
Copyright: Alvar Aalto Foundation

The most important Finnish architect of the 20th century, Alvar Aalto (1898-1976) was a central figure in international modernism. His greatest buildings, like the 1927 Viipuri Library and 1928 Paimio Sanatorium, fused the naturalism of Finnish romanticism with modernist ideals: as did his influential furniture and glassware.

By the 1950s, Alvar Aalto, the great Finnish architect, was one of the handful of people in Finland who were considered so important that, if they were late for a Finnair flight, the airline delayed take-off until they were safely on board. More often than not, Aalto did arrive late and Finnair passengers grew accustomed to waiting for him to board the aircraft. Aalto enjoyed this so much that, if he arrived on time, he instructed his chauffeur to drive around Helsinki Airport until he was late enough to stage a grand entrance.

Such aplomb was typical of Aalto who, even at the start of his career, had the chutzpah to style himself as a world-class architect. Born Hugo Alvar Henrik Aalto in 1898 in the Finnish town of Kuortane, he graduated in architecture from the Helsinki University of Technology in 1921 before assisting the Swedish architect Arvid Bjerke. Back

Location | Supporting the Design Museum | Design at the Design Museum | Digital Design Museum

Design at the
Design Museum

Alvar Aalto
Aluminium
Shin + Tomoko Azumi
Georg Baldele
Luis Barragán
Saul Bass
Leopold + Rudolf Blaschka
Andrew Blauvelt
Ronan + Erwan Bouroullec
Marcel Breuer
Daniel Brown
Joe Colombo
Joshua Davis
Design Laboratory
Tom Dixon
Charles + Ray Eames
Foundation 33
John Galliano
Arne Jacobsen
Hella Jongerius
M/M
J. Mays
Memphis
Mevis + Van Deursen

5

main_content[1] - Notepad

File   Edit   Format   View   Help

```
<style type="text/css">

<!--

     A { color: #000000; text-decoration: none; }

     A:hover { color: #000000; text-decoration: none }

     A:link { color: #000000; text-decoration: none }

     A:visited { color: #000000; text-decoration: none }

     .maintxt { font-size: 10px; font-family: Verdana, Arial, Helvetica,
sans-serif; color:#676767; font-weight: none;}

     .imgDescriptiontxt { font-size: 9px; font-family: Verdana, Arial,
Helvetica, sans-serif; color:#999999; font-weight: none;}

// -->

</style>
```

3 What's particularly impressive about the site is the way that it also provides a good deal of textual content—accessed through the final two links. Here you'll find an online archive of information about modern designers. Particularly striking is the use of a two-window design with the content

list always available down the right. Both windows turn off the browser's menus and toolbars to produce an effect that feels more like browsing an interactive CD-ROM—but it's all done with HTML.

4 *Open the main content page into its own window and you can see how simple the underlying layout is. Essentially, it's a two-column table with all the graphics down the left and all the text down the right. There's quite a bit of text here, so readability is an issue.*

5 *Take a look at the CSS formatting code and we can see exactly what we are dealing with. There are just two CSS styles: one for the image captions of Verdana at 9 pixels and in a light gray; and one for the body text of Verdana at 10 pixels in a darker gray. Setting text size as fixed pixels is a risk because the end user can't change it, but in this case they can't anyway since the browser menu bar is hidden. Ten pixels is also very tight—almost at the limit of easy readability, especially as gray against white has less contrast than black. It's a risk, but Verdana with its large x-height makes the most of every pixel and, at that size, its letter shapes are particularly modern: especially well suited for a site that's concerned with the latest design trends. It's a risk, but as with the logo it's one that pays off.*

Handling web type is never simple or straightforward, but the Design Museum site shows just what can be achieved. It's an excellent example of using every type technology at your disposal—bitmap, Flash, HTML, and CSS—and pushing the boundaries with each.

174 CSS2 & ABSOLUTE POSITIONING

To most users, CSS might seem like an excitingly new technology. In fact, the first CSS specification was released back in 1996—an absolute age ago in Web terms. The time since has largely been spent waiting for the browser and authoring application developers to catch on and add robust CSS support. Thankfully, critical mass has been achieved and CSS has gone mainstream.

The developers of CSS haven't sat on their laurels, however. They have used the intervening time to improve and expand the CSS specification. In 1998, this resulted in the release of the CSS2 specification. As well as adding minor tweaks to existing power and the mechanism for specifying downloadable fonts, CSS2 tackles two main areas of entirely new functionality.

The first is the ability to provide precise layout control. As we saw back in chapter two, the fluid and flowing nature of HTML makes it difficult to gain any control over your layout. We've seen how a way around this can be found using tables but, just like the deprecated <font> tag, this is awkward to edit and wasteful. In fact, more code is often spent defining the table grid than its contents.

The layout solution that the CSS developers have come up with is—as always—beautifully simple. Effectively, they've taken the existing <div> division tag that we put to good use in the last chapter, and turned it into an all-purpose container that can be used to precisely size and absolutely position your text and images.

The use of CSS2 absolute positioning offers huge potential for the Web designer wanting to take efficient and total control over their layouts. As such, it's hardly surprising to find that the main authoring applications have been quick to seize on the opportunity to offer DTP-style WYSIWYG control.

1

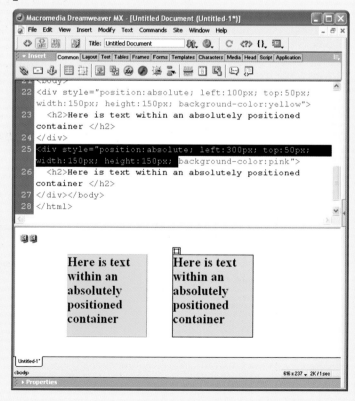

Cascading Style Sheets, level 2 CSS2 Specification

W3C Recommendation 12-May-1998

This version:
http://www.w3.org/TR/1998/REC-CSS2-19980512
Latest version:
http://www.w3.org/TR/REC-CSS2
Previous version:
http://www.w3.org/TR/1998/PR-CSS2-19980324
Editors:
Bert Bos <bbos@w3.org>
Håkon Wium Lie <howcome@w3.org>
Chris Lilley <chris@w3.org>
Ian Jacobs <ij@w3.org>

Abstract

This specification defines Cascading Style Sheets, level 2 (CSS2). CSS2 is a style sheet language that allows authors and users to attach style (e.g., fonts, spacing, and aural cues) to structured documents (e.g., HTML documents and XML applications). By separating the presentation style of documents from the content of documents, CSS2 simplifies Web authoring and site maintenance.

2

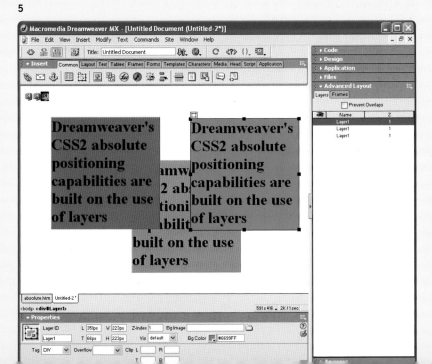

1 *The CSS2 specification is available from the w3 website, at www.w3.org/TR/REC-CSS2*

2 *To turn a <div> tag into a CSS2 container for type, all you need to do is to apply an inline style to it. To do this manually, set the {position} property to "absolute," then specify pixel measurements for the {left} and {top} properties to fix the box's top left hand corner. Do the same for the width and height properties to fix its size.*

3 *To position your text in FrontPage, you need to display the Positioning toolbar and select your text, then click on the Absolute Positioning icon and drag your container into the desired position.*

4 *In GoLive, you add floating boxes from the Objects palette and can precisely control them with the Inspector palette.*

5 *In Dreamweaver, <div> containers are called layers and can be added from the Insert toolbar, interactively resized and positioned, and then reordered and renamed with the dedicated Layers panel.*

176 CSS2 & ABSOLUTE POSITIONING 2

The potential of CSS2's absolute positioning is certainly exciting, but there's a serious problem. By tying CSS1 type formatting to the underlying HTML tag framework, we can set up a design that degrades reasonably gracefully with non-CSS supporting browsers. With absolute positioning, however, a page viewed in a non-CSS2 supporting browser, is likely to be an unholy mess!

Before using CSS2's absolute positioning, then, it's really important to know that your end user will see your page as intended. Until full browser support for CSS2 is universal, that means your only option is to produce two versions of a layout: one with absolute positioning, and one that is table based. You can then use a "browser-sniffing" script to recognize the CSS capabilities of your visitor's browser and direct them to the desired page.

Of course, creating two versions of every page and trying to keep them in synch is a lot of work for comparatively little gain. As such, until CSS2 support reaches critical mass, most designers will stick with the table-based layout approach, even though this is now officially deprecated.

Apart from precision, efficiency, and future-proofing, CSS2's absolute positioning has one further trick up its sleeve that table-based layouts just can't offer: scriptability. By giving each <div> container a unique ID, it's possible to control its position, visibility, and stacking-order via Javascript embedded in your code. Using this Dynamic HTML (DHTML), it's possible to set up animated layouts, where text layers fly in as a page loads, or even interactive layouts, where text and images update as the user moves the mouse over them.

This is exciting interactive power and for a high-impact home page, for example, it might well be worth putting CSS2 and DHTML to work already (just remember to redirect older browsers to a non-CSS alternative). The real excitement, though, will come when CSS2 browser support is universal and such dynamic power will be available for every page we create. By comparison, the printed page will seem static and uninspiring.

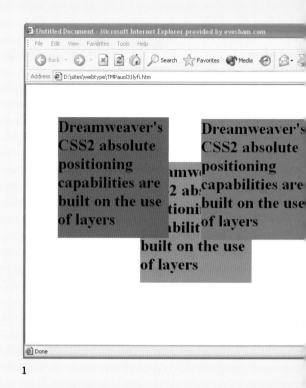

1

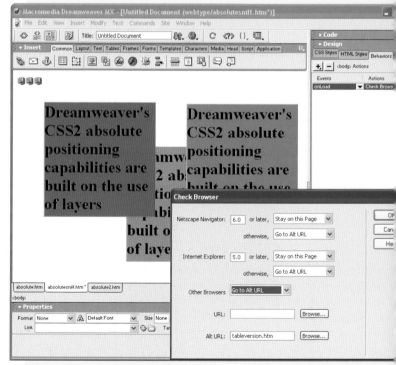

2

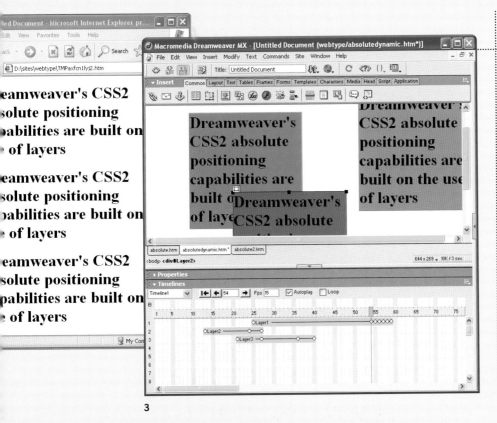

3

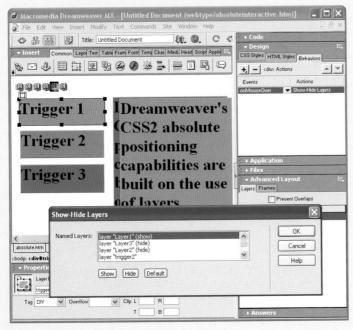

4

1 *When a browser ignores the CSS2 information, your carefully constructed layout will sadly fall to pieces.*

2 *Using Dreamweaver's Behaviors panel, you can add scripts to serve up pages according to the end user's browser's capabilities.*

3 *Most users aren't proficient in Javascript, but this isn't necessary with Dreamweaver, which offers dedicated Timeline-based handling.*

4 *Having layers fly around is certainly eye-catching, but it should be used sparingly. Much more engaging is the ability to add behaviors to layers to control when other layers are hidden or displayed. Working in this way, you can create rollover layouts, where the page content seems to update and interact as the user moves the mouse over the page.*

178 CSS2 MEDIA TYPES

Absolute positioning is the CSS2 feature that grabbed most headlines, but there's another innovation which could prove just as important for the web type expert—CSS media types.

So far, all our CSS-based type formatting has been based on the assumption that our pages will be displayed on a typical desktop computer system. But while that's certainly how most users browse the Web at the moment, it isn't necessarily going to be the case for the future.

To begin with, the rise of mobile phones and PDAs means that users will increasingly be accessing the Web on the move, via smaller handheld devices. At the same time, as the Web develops to become more of an entertainment platform, it's likely that we'll be interacting with the Web via a TV screen on the other side of the room. At the same time, users with limited vision will need to be catered for with designs that work aurally or even in Braille.

In other words, designing for the computer screen will be only one element of designing for the Web of the future—and not necessarily the most important. What we need is some way of targeting our designs to multiple possible destinations, and that's exactly what CSS2's media types provide.

Designing for different platforms will become increasingly important over time, but there's one media type that is crucial right now—the printed page. As we've seen repeatedly, designing for screen and page demand two very different approaches. Using the "print" media type lets us set up radically different style sheets to independently manage how our pages will appear on screen and on paper.

The Web's huge strength is that it is a universally accessible medium, but to reach its full potential, it has to become accessible to many different devices. Thanks to CSS2's introduction of media types, we'll be able to produce multi-purpose designs that are managed efficiently and centrally but which are tailored to make the most of each output destination's capabilities.

2

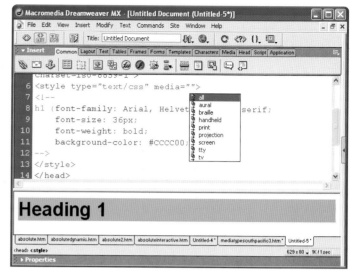

1

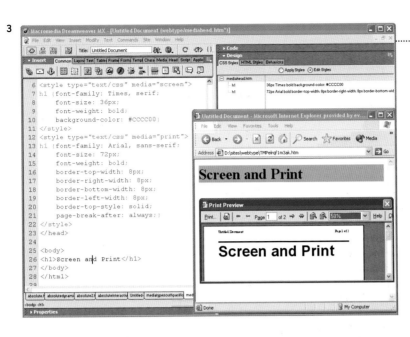

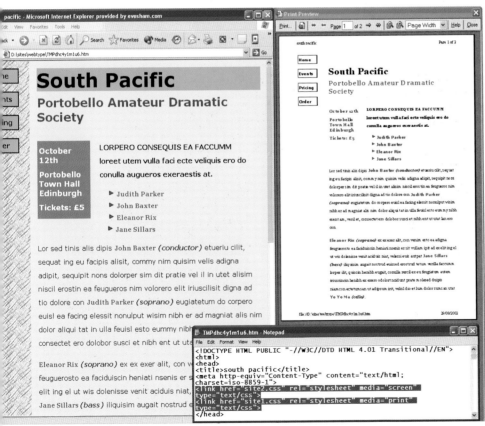

4

1 *In the future, we'll be accessing the Web via handheld devices and will have to design pages accordingly.*

2 *As always with CSS, the system is beautifully simple. All you need to do is set a media type attribute in the <style> tag or in the <link> tag to the external CSS stylesheet. If no media type is set, "screen" is assumed as the default.*

3 *By creating separate styles for screen and print, we can manage type and layout features accordingly, as shown here in Internet Explorer's main browser window and its Print Preview window.*

4 *In fact, simply by setting the media type for external style sheets, we can run two completely different designs in tandem. Here we've used the sans serif CSS file we created earlier for onscreen reading and the serif CSS for print.*

180 THE FUTURE: CSS3

Before it's worthwhile for the designer to begin using any CSS feature, we need to know that the end user will be able to benefit from it. This means that we have to wait until every common browser decides to support a feature before we first use it (or at least until such critical mass is reached that the onus shifts onto the end-user to upgrade their browser).

Unfortunately, this means that there's little pressure on the browser developer to ensure that the support that they do add is complete and reliable. Instead, the temptation is to throw in half-baked CSS support so that the feature-list looks good. And, as we saw with Navigator 4, it's far better not to support a feature at all rather than to half support it.

Thankfully, it's exactly this issue that the World Wide Web Consortium has chosen to address in its proposals for the next CSS specification: CSS3. Rather than adding new functionality, the main thrust in CSS3 is to improve support for the existing CSS1 and CSS2 functionality.

This is achieved by breaking down the specification into separate modules, each of which deals with a specific area, such as border formatting and absolute positioning. This means that rather than having to try and implement CSS functionality on all fronts simultaneously, the browser developers can concentrate their efforts on the modules they deem most important. In other words, there will be a rigor to the CSS3 specification, which has never existed before. It might not sound like much, but it's a fundamental advance. In the past, the final appearance of each page was ultimately at the mercy of the browser developers. With CSS3, there will finally be a recognized and universal standard, to which all future browsers can adhere.

Thanks to CSS3, the designer will finally be able to set up their type-based layouts and be confident of how they will appear on the screen.

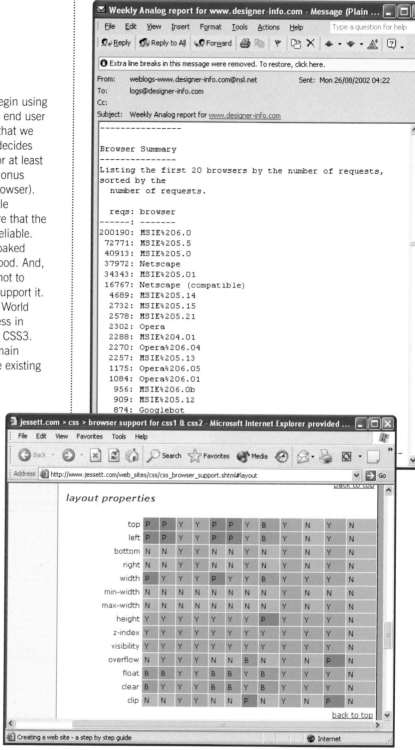

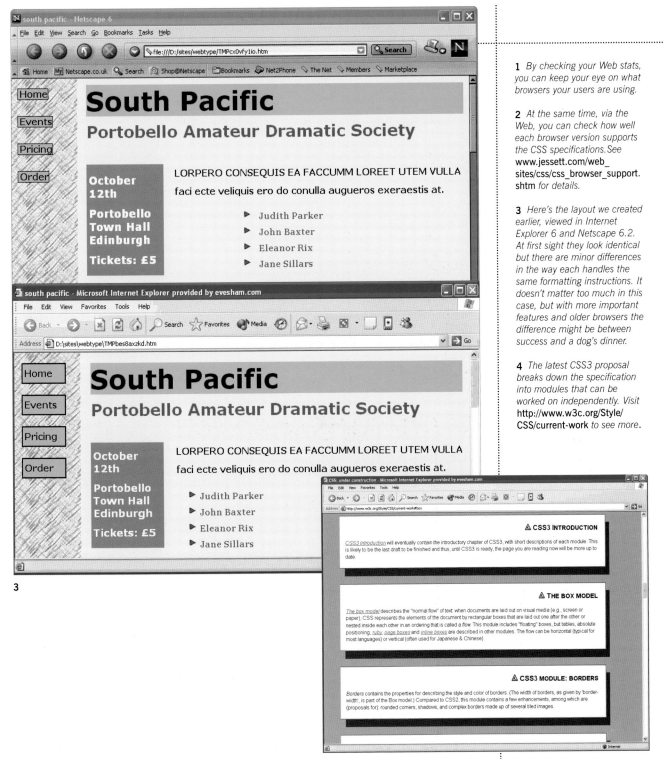

1 *By checking your Web stats, you can keep your eye on what browsers your users are using.*

2 *At the same time, via the Web, you can check how well each browser version supports the CSS specifications. See* **www.jessett.com/web_sites/css/css_browser_support.shtm** *for details.*

3 *Here's the layout we created earlier, viewed in Internet Explorer 6 and Netscape 6.2. At first sight they look identical but there are minor differences in the way each handles the same formatting instructions. It doesn't matter too much in this case, but with more important features and older browsers the difference might be between success and a dog's dinner.*

4 *The latest CSS3 proposal breaks down the specification into modules that can be worked on independently. Visit* **http://www.w3c.org/Style/CSS/current-work** *to see more.*

3

4

182 THE FUTURE: XML

Thanks to CSS, Web formatting is moving toward becoming far more rigorous and more powerful. So much so, that it's the underlying HTML framework which looks old-fashioned and under-powered. There are two main problems. As we saw earlier, HTML was originally designed around just a few tags that the browser applications were free to interpret as they saw fit. Nowadays, this free-and-easy approach has become a major stumbling block: HTML is just too sloppy for its own good.

What's needed is a stricter version of HTML, just as CSS3 is a stricter version of CSS2. And this is exactly what the World Wide Web Consortium has proposed with its XHTML (eXtensible HTML) specification. XHTML is a reworking of HTML based on the stricter XML (eXtensible Markup Language), in which every tag is closed and the syntax must be absolutely correct.

In fact, XHTML is itself eventually likely to prove a stepping-stone to the long-term future of the Web, which will be based on XML itself. The main advantage that this offers is that users can create their own tags for marking any content features they wish. Apart from their increasing rigor and extendability, the one other feature that both XHTML and XML provide is that they have absolutely nothing to say about formatting. In a way, this is a continuation of the back-to-basics shift—a return to Tim Berners-Lee's original vision of HTML as a purely content-based mark-up language.

How will we control the appearance of our type and pages? The answer, of course, is through a mark-up language dedicated to controlling the styling of that content, and the obvious candidate for the job is CSS.

1

1 *Dreamweaver makes it simple to convert existing HTML pages to conform to XHTML.*

2 *Under XML you can create your own tags for addresses, prices, quotes, names and anything else you can think of simply by wrapping an opening and closing tag around the text content.*

3 *Here's the XML file formatted with separate external CSS style sheets for onscreen display and for print.*

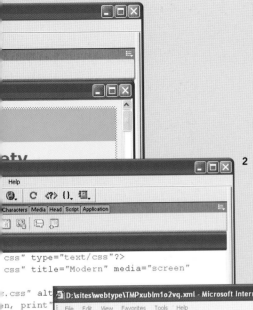

2

Where we stand

It might not seem like we have come a long way: even at the end of the book, we're still making use of the same core HTML tags that we put to use in the first project. Yet we have traveled far when we set out on this journey, we had no real control over our type's face, size, spacing, style, weight, alignment, margins, borders, or layout, and were effectively leaving all formatting to the end user's browser. Now, thanks to our understanding of the different versions of HTML, font embedding, and, especially CSS, we've gained serious control over all these factors, and in a supremely efficient and flexible way.

Now we know that we are on the right track. With XHTML and eventually XML working alongside CSS, we can see the future of Web type handling beginning to take shape. With quantum leaps in control and quality, the Web will finally be able to move into DTP-style territory and to match anything that the printed page has to offer. When this quality and control are added to the web page's existing strengths of near-free and near-instant publishing, near-free and near-universal access, and its inherently flexible, dynamic and interactive nature, it will be the printed page that looks underpowered.

The future for Web type-handling is bright indeed!

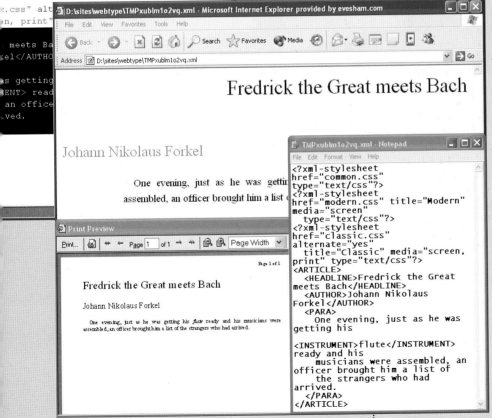

3

10

Reference

Glossary

Acrobat The application used to create Adobe's "portable document format" (PDF) file, where fonts and pictures are embedded in the document. Also used as shorthand for the format, and also refers to the program used to view PDFs.

antialias/antialiasing A technique of optically eliminating the jagged effect of bitmapped images or text reproduced on low-resolution devices such as monitors. This is achieved by adding pixels of an in-between tone—the edges of the object's color are blended with its background by averaging the density of the range of pixels involved.

ascender The part of a lowercase character which extends above its body ("x-height"), as in the letters b, d, f, h, k, l, t. .

ASCII acronym: American Standard Code for Information Interchange. A code that assigns a number to the 256 letters, numbers, and symbols (including carriage returns and tabs) that can be typed on a keyboard. ASCII is the cross-platform, computer-industry standard, text-only file format.

attribute (1) The specification applied to a character, box, or other item. Character attributes include font, size, style, color, shade, scaling, kerning, etc.

attribute (2) A characteristic of an HTML tag that is identified alongside the tag in order to describe it.

bandwidth The measure of the speed at which information is passed between two points. The broader the bandwidth, the faster data flows.

baseline The imaginary line, defined by the flat base of a lowercase letter such as "x," upon which the bases of all upper and lowercase letters apparently rest.

bevel A chamfered edge applied to type, buttons, or selections to lend them a 3D effect.

bitmap Strictly speaking, any text character or image composed of dots. A bitmap is a "map" describing the location and binary state (on or off) of "bits"; it defines the complete collection of pixels or dots that comprise an image (on a monitor, for example).

bitmapped font A bitmapped font is one in which the characters are made up of dots, or pixels, as distinct from an outline font which is drawn from vectors.

bowl The enclosed space in a text character, such as a b, g, o, q or p.

browser Program that enables the viewing or "browsing" of World Wide Web pages across the Internet.

bulleted list An HTML style for web pages in which a bullet precedes each item on a list.

character set The complete repertoire of letters, numbers, and symbols in a font design.

compression The technique of rearranging data so that it either occupies less space on disk or transfers faster between devices or on communication lines. Compression methods that don't lose data are referred to as "lossless," while "lossy" is used to describe methods in which some data is lost.

CSS abbr. Cascading Style Sheets. The name for a specification sponsored by the World Wide Web Consortium for overcoming the limitations imposed by "classic HTML." Web designers ("authors") have increasingly sought tools which would enable them to control every element of page design more tightly. CSS allows the designer to exercise greater control over typography and layout applying attributes such as font formats to paragraphs, parts of pages, or entire pages. Several style sheets can be applied to a single page, thus "cascading." .

CSS2 The second CSS specification most notable for its introduction of absolute positioning and media types. See CSS, CSS3.

CSS3 The current proposal for the next CSS specification breaks the markup language into more manageable modules. See CSS, CSS2.

deprecated The term applied to older versions of the HTML language or Web technology which are gradually being replaced or eradicated.

descender The part of a lower case character that extends below the baseline of the x-height, as in p, q, j and g,

dingbat The modern name for fonts of decorative symbols, traditionally called printer's "ornaments" or "arabesques".

dpi abbr. Dots Per Inch. A unit of measurement used to represent the resolution of devices such as printers and imagesetters and also, erroneously, monitors and images, whose resolution should more properly be expressed in pixels per inch (ppi). The closer the dots or pixels (the more there are to each inch) the better the quality. See resolution.

drop shadow A shadow projected onto the background behind an image or character, designed to "lift" the image or character off the surface of the page.

dynamic HTML A development of HTML which employs CSS and JavaScript to add enhanced features such as basic animations and highlighted buttons to Web pages without the need for a browser plug-in.

EOT abbr. Embedded Open Type font. A font format developed by Microsoft that enables fonts to be delivered over the Web. See OpenType.

export A feature provided by many applications which enables you to save a file in a format that can be used in another application.

file format The method in which a program arranges data so that it can be stored or used by itself or another application. JPEG, GIF and TIFF are all popular image file formats.

Flash Macromedia's application for creating vector graphics and animations for Web presentations. Flash generates small files, which are correspondingly quick to download and, being vector, are scalable to any dimension without an increase in the file size.

font A set of characters sharing the same typeface and size. See typeface.

GIF abbr.: graphics interchange format. One of the main bitmapped image formats used on the Internet, GIF is a 256-color format based on a "lossless" compression technique. It's small file sizes make it suitable for line images and other graphic elements, such as text.

Glyph The individual graphical symbol used to indicate a particular character in a typeface.

heading A formatting term used in HTML which determines the size at which text will be displayed in a WWW browser. There are six sizes, available usually referred to as H1, H2, H3, H4, H5, and H6.

helper application An application that assists a web browser in delivering or displaying information such as Acrobat PDF of Flash SWF files.

home page A World Wide Web term used to describe the main page or contents page on a particular site, which provides links to all the other pages on that site. It sometimes has the alternate meaning of the page that your own browser automatically links to when you launch it.

HTML abbr.: HyperText Markup Language. A comparatively simple system of "tags" (HTML is not a programming language) that specify type styles and sizes, the location of graphics, and other information required to construct a Web page. A recent version, HTML 4.0, incorporates DHTML and supports cascading style sheets.

HTML table A grid on a Web page consisting of rows and columns of cells allowing precise positioning of text, pictures, movie clips, or any other element. A table can be nested within another table. Tables offer a way of giving the appearance of multi-column layouts..

Hypertext A programming concept that links any single word or group of words to an unlimited number of others, typically text on a web page that has an embedded link to other documents or websites. Hypertext links are usually underlined and/or in a different color to the rest of the text, and are activated by clicking on them..

Internet The world-wide network of computers, providing individual and corporate users with access to the World Wide Web, e-mail, newsgroups, and more.

Internet Explorer A cross-platform web browser produced by Microsoft.

italic The sloping version of a roman type design deriving from cursive handwriting and calligraphic scripts, intended for textual emphasis.

JPEG This is a digital image file form format particularly suited to continuous tone images such as photographs. It uses a lossy compression algorithm to squeeze large images into smaller, more compact files. The Joint Photographers Expert Group first created the format.

kerning The adjustment of spacing between two characters to improve the overall look of the text.

leading The setting that defines the space that seperates two lines of type.

list element Text in a Web page which is displayed as a list and which is defined by the HTML tag <LI> (list item).

markup language A defined set of rules describing the way files are displayed by any particular method. In conventional Internet applications, HTML (and its extensions such as DHTML) is the principal language used for creating web pages.

monitor Your computer screen, or the unit that houses it. Variously referred to as screens, displays, VDUs, and VDTs. Monitors display images in color, grayscale, or monochrome, and are available in a variety of sizes (which are measured diagonally), ranging from 9in (229mm) to 21in (534mm) or more. Al-though most monitors use cathode-ray tubes, some contain liquid-crystal displays (LCDs), particularly portables and laptops and, more recently, gas plasma (large matrices of tiny, gas-filled glass cells).

Navigator A cross-platform Web browser produced by Netscape.

Netscape Company responsible for pioneering the web browser with its Navigator and Communicator products. Now part of AOL.

OpenType A superset of the existing TrueType and Type 1 formats, designed to provide support for type in print and onscreen and, with its compression technology, is also relevant to the Internet and the World Wide Web, since it allows fast downloading of type.

palette The subset of colors used to display a particular image. A GIF image, for example, has a palette of 256 colors, while a full-color JPEG photo may have a palette of over 16 million colors .

paragraph In an HTML document, a markup tag <P> used to define a new paragraph in text.

path A line, often invisible, which is used to control or constrain the flow of text. A path can be straight, curved or irregular, and the text often flows along the top of it.

PDF abbr.: portable document format. The cross-platform, cross-application page description format created by Adobe, which enables users of different applications and operating systems to view text-based documents.

pixel abbr.: picture element. The smallest component of any digitally generated image, including text, such as a single dot of light on a computer screen.

plug-in A small program that works in conjunction with a larger application to provide support for a particular function. To see a Flash animation, for example, you would need the Flash plug-in for your browser.

point The most common unit used for describing and setting the size of type. One point is 1/72 of an inch.

rasterize The electronic conversion of a vector graphic into a bitmap image. The process may introduce aliasing problems, but is often necessary when preparing vector images, including text, for use on the Web.

readability The ease and comfort with which a text can be read, particularly in the context of web pages..

resolution (1) The degree of quality, definition, or clarity with which an image or text is reproduced.

resolution (2) Monitor resolution, screen resolution The number of pixels across by pixels down. The three most common resolutions are 640 x 480, 800 x 600, and 1,024 x 768. The current standard Web page size is 800 x 600.

roman (type) A font design in which the characters are upright, as distinct from italic.

sans (serif) A typeface marked by the lack of serifs.

serif The small tick-marks at the end of letter shapes. A reminder of the days when all writing was done by hand, they remain a common feature in typefaces today.

smoothing The refinement of bitmapped images and text by a technique called "anti-aliasing" (adding pixels of an "in-between" tone).

source code In the context of the Internet, an alternative name for HTML.

stem The main vertical stroke in a text characters, such as a t, p or f.

SWF abbr.: Shockwave Flash Format. The file extension for a Macromedia Flash movie. See Flash.

tag The formal name for a markup language formatting command. A tag is switched on by placing a command inside angle brackets and switched off again by repeating the same command but inserting a forward slash before the command. For example, <bold> makes text that follows appear in bold and </bold> switches bold text off.

title Text which appears in the title bar of a web page.

TrueDoc A font format devised by the Bitstream Corporation which is completely independent of platform, operating system, application, resolution, and device.

TrueType This font was originated by Apple Computer's digital font technology, which was developed as an alternative to PostScript and is now used by both Apple and Microsoft for their respective operating systems.

Type 1 font The Adobe PostScript outline font technology which first introduced "hints" for improved rendering on-screen.

typeface The term (based on "face"—the printing surface of a metal type character) describing a particular type design of any size. Often used interchangeably—though mistakenly—with font. See font.

Typography The study and use of type based on its underlying graphical nature.

vector graphics Images made up of mathematically defined shapes, such as circles and rectangles, or complex paths built out of mathematically defined curves. Vector graphics images can be displayed at any size or resolution without loss of quality.

web authoring The process of writing (in HTML or XML format) documents for publishing on the World Wide Web. See World Wide Web (WWW)

web page A published HTML document on the World Wide Web. See website; World Wide Web (WWW).

website The address, location (on a server), and collection of documents and resources for any particular interlinked set of web pages.

WEFT abb.:Web embedding font tool. Microsoft's solution to the problem of downloading fonts without breach of copyright. WEFT does not require a plug-in. See also Truedoc.

white space The term describing areas of white in a design or layout that contain no text or images, but which form an integral part of the design.

World Wide Web The term used to describe the entire collection of web servers all over the world which are connected to the Internet. The term also describes the particular type of Internet access architecture which uses a combination of HTML and various graphic formats, such as GIF and JPEG, to publish formatted text which can be read by web browsers. Colloquially termed simply "the web" or, sometimes by the shorthand "W3."

World Wide Web Consortium The organization responsible for maintaining and managing standards across the Web. Often abbreviated as the W3C.

XML abbr.: Extensible Markup Language. An evolution (and probable successor) of HTML (the underlying language used on web pages), offering more sophisticated and rigorous control. XML allows the creation of user-defined tags, which expands the amount of information that can be provided about the data held in documents.

190

Useful Websites

www.microsoft.com/typography/ Like it or loathe it, Microsoft is the major player in software and browser development. It has also done a lot to improve Web type handling and this section of the main Microsoft site is devoted to screen-based typography.

www.wpdfd.com/wpdtypo.htm Wpdfd stands for Web Page Design For Designers and it's a good brief introduction to the main Web type issues.

hotwired.lycos.com/webmonkey/design/fonts/ The Webmonkey site offers an excellent all round exploration of web authoring. This section of the site deals with the particular issues raised by handling Web type.

www.w3.org/MarkUp/Guide/ To produce successful web pages you need to get to grips with HTML, and this single page introduction ensures you'll get off on the right foot.

www.w3schools.com/html A comprehensive online HTML tutorial with an invaluable reference for each HTML 4.01 tag.

www.w3.org/ The World Wide Web Consortium's site is the best place to find technical content such as the full HTML, XHTML and XML specifications.

www.autofx.com AutoFX is mainly known for its Photoshop add-ons, but it's also a superb source of free fonts, arranged into sixteen categories from artistic to whimsical.

http://www.webfontlist.com There are many other sources of free fonts on the Web. This site claims to be the most comprehensive listing available and provides both category-based and alphabetical access.

www.truedoc.com/ Home to Bitstream's TrueDoc, the pioneering font embedding technology.

www.microsoft.com/typography/web/embedding/weft3/ WEFT, the Web Embedding Font Tool, is Microsoft's solution for expanding Internet Explorer's web type horizons. You can download it for free from this page.

www.w3.org/Style/CSS/ The official home page for CSS (Cascading Style Sheets).It's technical, but everything you need to know is here.

hotwired.lycos.com/webmonkey/authoring/stylesheets/ The section of the excellent Webmonkey site dedicated to CSS and containing in-depth and accessible tutorials and articles.

www.webreview.com/style/ For more digestible information on using CSS in practice out in the real world this site is a must – especially its browser compatibility tables.

www.designer-info.com Over 200 reviews, articles and tutorials on all the latest design software for Web and print written by yours truly. What more can I say?

Acknowledgments

Special thanks and love to Jane for all her support.